The Age of Dryden

GOLDENTREE BIBLIOGRAPHIES

In Language and Literature

under the series editorship of

O. B. Hardison, Jr.

The Age
of Dryden

compiled by

Donald F. Bond

The University of Chicago

AHM Publishing Corporation
Northbrook, Illinois 60062

PRINTED IN THE UNITED STATES OF AMERICA

783

Second Printing

Preface

THE FOLLOWING BIBLIOGRAPHY is intended for graduate and advanced undergraduate students who desire a convenient guide to scholarship on English literature of the Restoration period (1660–1700). The listing is necessarily selective, but every effort has been made to indicate the significant work done on major authors and topics, with emphasis on books and articles of more recent date. The bibliography attempts to steer a middle course between the brief lists provided by the average textbook and the exhaustive references in the professional bibliographies. It should be of assistance to the student in writing reports and term papers, preparing for examinations, and doing independent reading.

The user should amplify his study here by turning to such indispensable bibliographical tools as the *Cambridge Bibliography of English Literature* (CBEL), the *Dictionary of National Biography* (DNB), and Watt's *Bibliotheca Britannica*, as well as the three annual bibliographies covering the entire field of English literature—the *Year's Work in English Studies*, the *MHRA Annual Bibliography*, and the *MLA International Bibliography*. In addition to these guides, the student of this period has available the annual critical survey founded by R. S. Crane ("English Literature, 1660–1800: A Current Bibliography"), which has appeared since 1926 in the *Philological Quarterly*. The *Johnsonian News Letter*, published from 1940 by James L. Clifford at Columbia University, is very useful, since it also covers the age of Dryden.

Attention is called to the following features in the present bibliography.

(1) Extra margin on each page permits listing of library call numbers of often-used items.

(2) Space at the bottom of every page permits inclusion of additional entries; and blank pages for notes also follow the final entry.

v

(3) Two indexes, one of subjects and one of authors, follow the bibliography proper.

An asterisk following an entry indicates a work of special importance in the field. The dagger (†) following an entry means that the item is available in a paperback edition. For books, London is to be assumed as place of publication unless otherwise given. The following abbreviations are used for *Festschriften*.

Campbell Festschrift. *Essays Critical and Historical Dedicated to Lily B. Campbell. By Members of the Department of English, University of California.* Berkeley, 1950.

Jones Festschrift. *The Seventeenth Century: Studies in the History of English Thought and Literature from Bacon to Pope, by Richard Foster Jones and Others Writing in his Honor.* Stanford, 1951. Repr. 1965.†

McKillop Festschrift. *Restoration and Eighteenth-Century Literature: Essays in Honor of Alan Dugald McKillop.* Ed. Carroll Camden. Chicago, 1963.

MacMillan Festschrift. *Essays in English Literature of the Classical Period Presented to Dougald MacMillan.* Ed. Daniel W. Patterson and Albrecht B. Strauss. Chapel Hill, 1967.

Monk Festschrift. *Studies in Criticism and Aesthetics, 1660–1800: Essays in Honor of Samuel Holt Monk.* Ed. Howard Anderson and John S. Shea. Minneapolis, 1967.

Nicolson Festschrift. *Reason and the Imagination: Studies in the History of Ideas, 1600–1800.* Ed. J. A. Mazzeo. New York and London, 1962.

Pinto Festschrift. *Renaissance and Modern Essays Presented to Vivian de Sola Pinto in Celebration of His Seventieth Birthday.* Ed. G. R. Hibbard. 1966.

Willey Festschrift. *The English Mind: Studies in the English Moralists Presented to Basil Willey.* Ed. Hugh Sykes Davies and George Watson. Cambridge, 1964.

Symbols for journals and series follow the standard forms used in the *PMLA* bibliographies. The symbols and their meanings are as follows:

ARS	Augustan Reprint Society
AS	Annals of Science
CL	Comparative Literature
CLAJ	College Language Association Journal
DramS	Drama Survey

DUJ	Durham University Journal
EA	Études Anglaises
E&S	Essays and Studies by Members of the English Association
ECS	Eighteenth Century Studies
EDH	Essays by Divers Hands
EHR	English Historical Review
EIC	Essays in Criticism
EL	Everyman's Library
ELH	Journal of English Literary History
ELN	English Language Notes
EML	English Men of Letters
ES	English Studies
ESA	English Studies in Africa
HLB	Harvard Library Bulletin
HLQ	Huntington Library Quarterly
HSNPL	Harvard Studies and Notes in Philology and Literature
IJES	Indian Journal of English Studies
JBS	Journal of British Studies
JEGP	Journal of English and Germanic Philology
JHI	Journal of the History of Ideas
JMH	Journal of Modern History
JWCI	Journal of the Warburg and Courtauld Institute
MLN	Modern Language Notes
MLQ	Modern Language Quarterly
MLR	Modern Language Review
MP	Modern Philology
N&Q	Notes and Queries
PBA	Proceedings of the British Academy
PBSA	Papers of the Bibliographical Society of America
PLL	Papers on Language and Literature
PLPLS–LHS	Proceedings of the Leeds Philosophical and Literary Society, Literary and Historical Section
PMLA	Publications of the Modern Language Association of America
PQ	Philological Quarterly
QJS	Quarterly Journal of Speech
RAA	Revue Anglo-Américaine
RBPH	Revue Belge de Philologie et d'Histoire
REL	Review of English Literature
RECTR	Restoration and Eighteenth-Century Theatre Research
RES	Review of English Studies
RLC	Revue de Littérature Comparée
RLV	Revue des Langues Vivantes
RMS	Renaissance and Modern Studies
RRestDS	Regents Restoration Drama Series
RS	Research Studies of the State College of Washington
SB	Studies in Bibliography
SEL	Studies in English Literature, 1500–1900
SN	Studia Neophilologica

SoRA	Southern Review: An Australian Journal of Literary Studies
SF&R	Scholars' Facsimiles and Reprints
SP	Studies in Philology
TCBS	Transactions of the Cambridge Bibliographical Society
TLS	[London] Times Literary Supplement
TSL	Tennessee Studies in Literature
TSLL	Texas Studies in Literature and Language
UMSLL	University of Michigan Studies in Language and Literature
UTQ	University of Toronto Quarterly
WBEP	Wiener Beiträge zur Englischen Philologie
WC	World's Classics
WTW	Writers and Their Work

NOTE: The publisher and compiler invite suggestions for additions to future editions of this bibliography.

Contents

CONTENTS

I

Bibliography and Surveys of Scholarship

(London, and Paris for French books, is to be assumed as place of publication, unless otherwise noted.)

1 WING, Donald G. *A Short-Title Catalogue of Books Printed in England, Scotland, Ireland, Wales, and British America, and of English Books Printed in Other Countries, 1641–1700.* 3 vols. New York, 1945–51.

2 CLIFFORD, James L. "The Eighteenth Century." *Contemporary Literary Scholarship: A Critical Review,* ed. Lewis Leary. New York, 1958, chap. vi. [In spite of its title, this deals also with Restoration literature. The chapter on the seventeenth century in the same volume deals mainly with Donne and Milton.]

3 CLIFFORD, James L. "The Eighteenth Century," *MLQ,* 26(1965):111–34.

4 GREENE, DONALD J. "Recent Studies in the Restoration and Eighteenth Century." *SEL,* 1(1961):115–41. [Continued annually, by different scholars, in the Summer issue of *SEL.*]

5 STAMM, Rudolf. *Englische Literatur.* "Prosa und Dichtung im 17. Jahrhundert," pp. 141–98; "Theater und Drama zwischen 1660 und 1800," pp. 199–216. Bern, 1957.†

Surveys and Reference Works

6 BAUGH, Albert C., ed. *A Literary History of England.* Book III: *The Restoration and Eighteenth Century (1660–1789),* by George Sherburn. New York, 1948. Rev. ed. by Donald F. Bond. New York, 1967.*†

7 BREDVOLD, Louis I. "*The Literature of the Restoration and Eighteenth Century.*" *A History of English Literature,* ed. Hardin Craig. New York, 1950, pp. 343–459.†

8 BURTON, K[athleen] M. P. *Restoration Literature.* 1958.

9 FORD, Boris, ed. *From Dryden to Johnson.* Vol. IV: *Pelican Guide to English Literature,* 1957.† [Essays by various hands, with Bibliographical Supplement.]

10 GARNETT, Richard. *The Age of Dryden.* 1895.

11 GRIERSON, H. J. C. *Cross-Currents in English Literature of the XVIIth Century.* . . . 1929.†

12 KUNITZ, Stanley J., and Howard HAYCRAFT. *British Authors before 1800: A Biographical Dictionary.* New York, 1952.

1 LEGOUIS, E., and L. CAZAMIAN. *Histoire de la littérature anglaise.* Book VI: *La Littérature de la Restauration, 1660–1702,* by Louis Cazamian. Paris, 1924.* [English translation by W. D. MacInnes and the Author, 1927, and later editions.]

2 McKILLOP, Alan D. *English Literature from Dryden to Burns.* New York, 1948.

3 SCHILLING, Bernard N., ed. *Essential Articles for the Study of English Augustan Backgrounds.* Hamden, Conn., 1961.

4 SUTHERLAND, James. *Oxford History of English Literature.* Vol. 6: *English Literature of the Late Seventeenth Century.* Oxford, 1969.*

5 WARD, A. W., and A. R. WALLER, eds. *Cambridge History of English Literature.* Vol. VIII: *The Age of Dryden.* Cambridge and New York, 1912.

Historical Background

6 ASHLEY, Maurice. *England in the Seventeenth Century, 1603–1714.* 1952.†

7 BROWNING, Andrew, ed. *English Historical Documents.* Vol. III: *1660–1714.* 1953.

8 CLARK, George N. *The Later Stuarts, 1660–1714.* Oxford, 1934; 2nd ed. rev., Oxford, 1955.*

9 DAVIES, Godfrey. *Bibliography of British History: Stuart Period, 1603–1714.* Oxford, 1928.

10 FEILING, Keith. *A History of the Tory Party, 1640–1714.* Oxford, 1924.

11 GROSE, Clyde L. *A Select Bibliography of British History, 1660–1760.* Chicago, 1939.

12 GUNN, J. A. W. *Politics and the Public Interest in the Seventeenth Century.* 1969.

13 HALEY, K. H. D. *The First Earl of Shaftesbury.* 1968.

14 MACAULAY, Thomas Babington. *The History of England from the Accession of James II.* 1849–61. [Ed. C. H. Firth. 6 vols. 1913–15; in *EL,* 3 vols, 1906.]

15 OGG, David. *England in the Reign of Charles II,* 2 vols. Oxford, 1934; 2nd ed., Oxford, 1956.†

16 OGG, David. *England in the Reigns of James II and William III.* Oxford, 1955.†

17 PLUMB, J. H. *The Growth of Political Stability in England, 1675–1725.* 1967.

18 ROWSE, A. L. *The Early Churchills: An English Family.* 1956.

19 STONE, T[hora] G. *England under the Restoration (1660–1688).* 1923.

1 SUTHERLAND, James. "The Impact of Charles II on Restoration Literature." *McKillop Festschrift*, pp. 251–63.

2 WALCOTT, Robert. "The Later Stuarts (1660–1714): Significant Work of the Last Twenty Years (1939–1959)." *Changing Views on British History: Essays on Historical Writing since 1939*, ed. Elizabeth C. Furber, Cambridge, Mass., 1966, pp. 160–80.

Social and Cultural Background
(London is to be assumed as place of publication, unless otherwise noted.)

3 BELJAME, Alexandre. *Men of Letters and the English Public in the Eighteenth Century*. Trans. E. O. Lorimer. 1948. [Original French ed., 1881. Chapters I and II (pp. 1–211) deal with the profession of letters during the Restoration period.]

4 BRETT-JAMES, Norman G. *The Growth of Stuart London*. 1935.

5 BRYANT, Arthur. *The England of Charles II*. 1934.

6 BURTON, Elizabeth. *The Pageant of Stuart England*. New York, 1962.

7 CLARKE, M. L. *Classical Education in Britain, 1500–1900*. Cambridge, 1959.

8 DELANY, Paul. *British Autobiography in the Seventeenth Century*. New York and London, 1969.

9 DOUGLAS, David C. *English Scholars, 1660–1730*. 1939. Rev. ed., 1951.

10 FUSSELL, G. E., and V. G. B. ATWATER. "Travel and Topography in Seventeenth-Century England: A Bibliography of Sources for Social and Economic History." *The Library*, 4th ser., 13 (1932): 292–311.

11 HOLE, Christina. *The English Housewife in the Seventeenth Century*. 1953.

12 LILLYWHITE, Bryant. *London Coffee Houses: A Reference Book*. 1963.

13 McLACHLAN, H[erbert]. *English Education under the Test Acts, Being the History of the Non-Conformist Academies, 1662–1820*. Manchester, 1931.

14 MASON, John E. *Gentlefolk in the Making: Studies in the History of English Courtesy Literature and Related Topics from 1531 to 1774*. Philadelphia, 1935.

15 NOYES, Gertrude E. *Bibliography of Courtesy and Conduct Books in Seventeenth-Century England*. New Haven, 1937.

16 PARKES, Joan. *Travels in England in the Seventeenth Century*. 1925.

17 PIMLOTT, John A. R. *The Englishman's Holiday: A Social History*. 1947.

1 PLOMER, Henry R., and others. *A Dictionary of the Printers and Booksellers Who Were at Work in England, Scotland and Ireland from 1668 to 1725*. 1922.

2 REYNOLDS, Myra. *The Learned Lady in England, 1650–1760*. Boston, 1920.

3 RUBINI, Dennis. *Court and Country, 1688–1702*. 1968.

4 SCHÜCKING, L[evin] L. *Die Familie in Puritanismus: Studien über Familie und Literatur in England im 16., 17. und 18. Jahrhundert*. Leipzig, 1929. 2nd ed. rev.: *Die puritanische Familie im literarsoziologischer Sicht*. Bern, 1964.

5 SMITH, J. W. Ashley. *The Birth of Modern Education: The Contribution of the Dissenting Academies, 1660–1800*. London and Chicago, 1954.

6 TROTTER, Eleanor. *Seventeenth Century Life in the Country Parish*. Cambridge, 1919. Repr. 1968.

7 USTICK, W. Lee. "Advice to a Son: A Type of Seventeenth-Century Conduct Book." *SP*, 29(1932):409–41.

8 USTICK, W. Lee. "Changing Ideals of Aristocratic Character and Conduct in Seventeenth-Century England." *MP*, 30(1932):147–66.

9 WALKER, J. "The Censorship of the Press during the Reign of Charles II." *History*, n.s. 35(1950):219–38.

10 WILES, R. M. *Serial Publication in England before 1750*. Cambridge, 1957.

Literary Criticism

Collections

11 ELLEDGE, Scott, and Donald SCHIER, eds. *The Continental Model: Selected French Critical Essays of the Seventeenth Century in English Translation*. Minneapolis, 1960.

12 SPINGARN, J. E., ed. *Critical Essays of the Seventeenth Century*. 3 vols. Oxford, 1908–9. Repr., Bloomington, Ind., 1957.

General Studies

13 ALLISON, Alexander W. *Toward an Augustan Poetic: Edmund Waller's "Reform" of English Poetry*. Lexington, Ky., 1962.

14 ATKINS, J. W. H. *English Literary Criticism: 17th and 18th Centuries*. 1951.†

15 BOND, Donald F. " 'Distrust' of Imagination in English Neo-classicism." *PQ*, 14(1935):54–69.

1 BRAY, René. *La Formation de la doctrine classique en France.* 1927.

2 BREDVOLD, Louis I. "The Rise of English Classicism: Study in Methodology." *CL*, 2(1950):253–68.

3 BRONSON, B. H. "When Was Neoclassicism?" *Monk Festschrift*, pp. 13–35.

4 CLARK, A. F. B. *Boileau and the French Classical Critics in England (1660–1830).* Paris, 1925.

5 CRANE, R. S. "English Neo-Classical Criticism: An Outline Sketch." *Dictionary of World Literature*, ed. Joseph T. Shipley. New York, 1943, pp. 193–203. Repr. in *Critics and Criticism, Ancient and Modern*, ed. R. S. Crane. Chicago, 1952, pp. 372–88.*

6 CRANE, R. S. "On Writing the History of English Criticism, 1650–1800." *UTQ*, 22(1953):376–91. Repr. in R. S. Crane, *The Idea of the Humanities and Other Essays Critical and Historical*. Chicago, 1967, II, 157–75.

7 DRAPER, John W. "The Rise of English Neo-Classicism." *RAA*, 10(1933): 399–409.

8 ERSKINE-HILL, Howard. "Augustans on Augustanism: England, 1655–1759." *RMS*, 11(1967):55–83.*

9 GALLAWAY, Francis. *Reason, Rule, and Revolt in English Classicism.* New York, 1940. Repr., Lexington, Ky., 1966.†

10 GOSSE, Edmund. *From Shakespeare to Pope: An Inquiry into the Causes and Phenomena of the Rise of Classical Poetry in England.* Cambridge, 1885.

11 HAMILTON, K[enneth] G. *The Two Harmonies: Poetry and Prose in the Seventeenth Century.* Oxford, 1963.

12 JONES, R. F. "The Moral Sense of Simplicity." *Studies in Honor of Frederick W. Shipley* (Saint Louis, 1942), pp. 265–87.

13 KORSHIN, Paul J. "The Evolution of Neo-classical Poetics: Cleveland, Denham, and Waller as Poetic Theorists." *ECS*, 2(1968):102–37.

14 MARKS, Emerson R. *Relativist and Absolutist: The Early Neoclassical Debate in England.* New Brunswick, N.J., 1955.

15 MARKS, Emerson R. *The Poetics of Reason. English Neoclassical Criticism.* New York, 1968.†

16 MAUROCORDATO, Alexandre. *La Critique classique en Angleterre de la Restauration à la mort de Joseph Addison: Essai de définition.* 1964.*

17 OGDEN, H. V. S. "The Principles of Variety and Contrast in Seventeenth Century Aesthetics, and Milton's Poetry." *JHI*, 10(1949):159–82.

18 PRICE, Martin. *To the Palace of Wisdom: Studies in Order and Energy from Dryden to Blake.* Garden City, New York, 1964.

19 SHARP, Robert L. *From Donne to Dryden: The Revolt against Metaphysical Poetry.* Chapel Hill, 1940.

1 SIMON, Irène. "Critical Terms in Restoration Translations from the French." *RBPH*, 42–43(1964–65):902–26.

2 SPINGARN, J. E. "The Origins of Modern Criticism." *MP*, 1(1904):477–96.

3 THORPE, Clarence DeWitt. *The Aesthetic Theory of Thomas Hobbes.* Ann Arbor, 1940.

4 VINES, Sherard. *The Course of English Classicism.* 1930.

5 WATSON, George. "Hobbes and the Metaphysical Conceit." *JHI*, 16(1955): 558–62. [See also *JHI*, 17(1956):418–21.]

6 WILLIAMSON, George. *The Proper Wit of Poetry.* 1961.

7 WILLIAMSON, George. "The Restoration Revolt against Enthusiasm." *SP*, 30(1933):571–603. Repr. in *Seventeenth-Century Contexts*, 1960, pp. 202–39.

8 WOOD, Paul Spencer. "Native Elements in English Neo-Classicism." *MP*, 24(1926):201–08.

9 WOOD, Paul Spencer. "The Opposition to Neo-Classicism in England between 1660 and 1700." *PMLA*, 43(1928):182–97.

10 YOUNGREN, William H. "Generality, Science and Poetic Language in the Restoration." *ELH*, 35(1968):158–87.

The Reform of Prose Style

11 ADOLPH, Robert. *The Rise of Modern Prose Style.* Cambridge, Mass., 1968.

12 BENNETT, Joan. "An Aspect of the Evolution of Seventeenth-Century Prose." *RES*, 17(1941):281–97.

13 CHRISTENSEN, Francis. "John Wilkins and the Royal Society's Reform of Prose Style." *MLQ*, 7(1946):179–87, 279–90.

14 CROLL, Morris W. "Attic Prose: Lipsius, Montaigne, Bacon." *Schelling Anniversary Papers.* New York, 1923, pp. 117–50.

15 CROLL, Morris W. " 'Attic Prose' in the Seventeenth Century." *SP*, 18(1921):79–128.

16 CROLL, Morris W. "The Baroque Style in Prose." *Studies in English Philology: A Miscellany in Honor of Frederick Klaeber.* Minneapolis, 1929, pp. 427–56.

17 CROLL, Morris W. "The Cadence of English Oratorical Prose." *SP*, 16(1919):1–55.

18 CROLL, Morris W. "Juste Lipse et le movement anticicéronien à la fin du XVIᵉ et au début du XVIIᵉ siècle." *Revue du Seizième Siècle*, 2(1914):200–42.

19 CROLL, Morris W. "Muret and the History of 'Attic' Prose." *PMLA*, 39(1924):254–309. [These articles by Croll are reprinted, with introductions and additional references, in *Style, Rhetoric, and Rhythm: Essays by Morris W. Croll*, ed. J. Max Patrick and Robert O. Evans, with John M. Wallace and R. J. Schoeck. Princeton, 1966.]†

1   FISCH, Harold. "The Puritans and the Reform of Prose Style." *ELH*, 20(1952):229–48.

2   HOWELLS, A. C. "*Res et Verba*: Words and Things." *ELH*, 13(1946):131–42.

3   JONES, Richard F. "The Attack on Pulpit Eloquence in the Restoration: An Episode in the Development of the Neo-Classical Standard for Prose." *JEGP*, 30(1931):188–217.

4   JONES, Richard F. "Science and English Prose Style in the Third Quarter of the Seventeenth Century." *PMLA*, 45(1930):977–1009.

5   JONES, Richard F. "Science and Language in England of the Mid-Seventeenth Century." *JEGP*, 31(1932):315–31. [These articles by Jones are reprinted in the *Jones Festschrift*.]

6   JONES, Richard F. *The Triumph of the English Language: A Survey of Opinions concerning the Vernacular from the Introduction of Printing to the Restoration*. Stanford, 1953.

7   KRAPP, George Philip. *The Rise of English Literary Prose*. New York, 1915.

8   MACDONALD, Hugh. "Another Aspect of Seventeenth-Century Prose." *RES*, 19(1943):33–43.

9   PURPUS, Eugene R. "The 'Plain, Easy, and Familiar Way': The Dialogue in English Literature, 1660–1725." *ELH*, 17(1950):47–58.

10 SAINTSBURY, George. *A History of English Prose Rhythm*. 1912.

11 TIETJE, Hans. "Le Style baroque." *Revue dè Synthèse*, 9(1935):116–22.

12 WILLIAMSON, George. *The Senecan Amble: A Study in Prose Style from Bacon to Collier*. London and Chicago, 1951.*†

13 WILSON, F. P. *Seventeenth Century Prose: Five Lectures*. Berkeley, 1960.

Dryden, John (1631–1700)

(London is to be assumed as place of publication, unless otherwise noted.)

Collected Works

14 *Dramatic Works*, ed. Montague Summers. 6 vols. 1931–32.

15 *Four Comedies*, ed. L. A. Beaurline and Fredson Bowers. Chicago, 1968. [*Secret Love, Marriage à-la-Mode, Sir Martin Mar-All, An Evening's Love*.]

16 *Four Tragedies*, ed. L. A. Beaurline and Fredson Bowers. Chicago, 1968. [*All for Love, Don Sebastian, The Indian Emperour, Aureng-Zebe*.]

1 *Hymns Attributed to John Dryden*, ed. George R. Noyes and George R. Potter. Berkeley, 1937.

2 *Letters*, ed. Charles E. Ward. Durham, N.C., 1942. [See also John Barnard, "The Dates of Six Dryden Letters," *PQ*, 42 (1963), 396–403; R. G. Howarth, "Dryden's Letters," *ESA*, 1 (1958), 184–94.]

3 *Poems*, ed. James Kinsley. 4 vols. Oxford, 1958. [One-volume edition: *Poems and Fables*, 1962.]

4 *Poetical Works*, ed. George R. Noyes. Boston, 1908; rev. ed., 1950.

5 *Prologues and Epilogues*, ed. William B. Gardner. New York, 1951.

6 *Songs*, ed. Cyrus L. Day. Cambridge, Mass., 1932.

7 *Works*, ed. H. T. Swedenberg, Jr., and Vinton A. Dearing, Berkeley, 1956–. Vol. I: *Poems, 1649–1680*, ed. E. N. Hooker *et al.*, 1956. Vol. VIII: *Plays: The Wild Gallant, The Rival Ladies, The Indian Queen*, ed. John Harrington Smith and Dougald MacMillan, 1962. Vol. IX: *Plays: The Indian Emperour, Secret Love, Sir Martin Mar-All*, ed. John Loftis and Vinton A. Dearing, 1966.

Selections

8 *The Best of Dryden*, ed. Louis I. Bredvold. New York, 1933.

9 *Poems*, selected by Bonamy Dobrée. (EL.) 1934.

Bibliographies and Concordances

10 DOBRÉE, Bonamy. *John Dryden*. (WTW). 1956.

11 LEGOUIS, P. "Ouvrages récents sur Dryden." *EA*, 17(1964):148–58.

12 MACDONALD, Hugh. *John Dryden: A Bibliography of Early Editions and of Drydeniana*. Oxford, 1939. [See James M. Osborn in *MP*, 39(1941–42):69–98; 197–212; 313–19.]

13 MONK, Samuel H. *John Dryden: A List of Critical Studies published from 1895 to 1948*. Minneapolis, 1950. [Reviewed by W. R. Keast in *MP*, 48(1951):205–10.]

14 MONTGOMERY, Guy. *Concordance to the Poetical Works of John Dryden*. Berkeley, 1957.

General Studies

15 ADAMS, Percy G. " 'Harmony of Numbers': Dryden's Alliteration, Consonance, Assonance." *TSLL*, 9(1967):333–43.

1 BLAIR, Joel. "Dryden's Ceremonial Hero." *SEL*, 9(1969):379–93.

2 BREDVOLD, Louis I. *The Intellectual Milieu of John Dryden: Studies in Some Aspects of Seventeenth-Century Thought.* Ann Arbor, 1934.†

3 BROWER, Reuben. "Dryden and the 'Invention' of Pope." *McKillop Festschrift*, pp. 211–33.

4 CRAIG, Hardin. "Dryden's Lucian." *Classical Philology*, 16(1921):141–63.

5 DAVISON, Dennis. *Dryden.* 1968.

6 ELIOT, T. S. *Homage to John Dryden: Three Essays on Poetry of the Seventeenth Century.* (Hogarth Essays.) 1924.

7 ELIOT, T. S. *John Dryden: The Poet, the Dramatist, the Critic.* New York, 1932.

8 EMERSON, Oliver F. "John Dryden and a British Academy." *PBA*, 10(1921):45–58.

9 EMERSON, Oliver F. "Dryden and the English Academy." *MLR*, 20(1925): 189–90.

10 EMSLIE, McD. "Dryden's Couplets: Imagery Vowed to Poverty." *Critical Quarterly*, 2(1960):51–57.

11 EMSLIE, McD. "Dryden's Couplets: Wit and Conversation." *EIC*, 11(1961):264–73.

12 FREEDMAN, Morris. "Dryden's 'Memorable Visit' to Milton." *HLQ*, 18(1955):99–108.

13 GARDNER, William B. "John Dryden's Interest in Judicial Astrology." *SP*, 47(1950):506–21.

14 HAM, Roswell G. "Dryden versus Settle." *MP*, 25(1928):409–16.

15 HAMILTON, K. G. *John Dryden and the Poetry of Statement.* Brisbane, 1967; East Lansing, Mich., 1969.

16 HARTH, Phillip. *Contexts of Dryden's Thought.* Chicago, 1968.*

17 HEMPHILL, George. "Dryden's Heroic Line." *PMLA*, 72(1957):863–79.

18 HOFFMAN, Arthur W. *John Dryden's Imagery.* Gainesville, Fla., 1962.

19 HORSMAN, E. A. "Dryden's French Borrowings." *RES*, n.s. 1(1950):346–51.

20 JEFFERSON, D. W. "Aspects of Dryden's Imagery." *EIC*, 4(1954):20–41.

21 KING, Bruce. "Dryden's Ark: The Influence of Filmer." *SEL*, 7(1967):403–14.

22 KINSLEY, James. "Dryden and the Art of Praise." *ES*, 34(1953):57–64.

23 KINSLEY, James. "Dryden and the *Encomium Musicae.*" *RES*, n.s. 4(1953):263–67.

24 LEGOUIS, P. "La Religion dans l'oeuvre de Dryden avant 1682." *RAA*, 9(1932):383–92, 525–36.

1   LUBBOCK, Alan. *The Character of John Dryden.* (Hogarth Essays.) 1925.

2   McFADDEN, George. "Dryden and the Numbers of His Native Tongue." *Essays and Studies in Language and Literature.* Pittsburgh, 1964, pp. 87–109.

3   MINER, Earl. "Dryden and the Issue of Human Progress." *PQ*, 40(1961): 120–29.

4   MINER, Earl. "Dryden as Prose Controversialist: His Role in *A Defence of the Royal Papers.*" *PQ*, 43(1964):412–19.

5   MINER, Earl. *Dryden's Poetry.* Bloomington, Ind., 1967.*

6   MORGAN, Edwin. "Dryden's Drudging." *Cambridge Journal*, 6(1953):414–29.

7   NICOLL, Allardyce. *Dryden and His Poetry.* 1923.

8   OSBORN, James M. *John Dryden: Some Biographical Facts and Problems.* New York, 1940. Rev. ed., Gainesville, Fla., 1965.*

9   PINTO, V. de Sola. "Rochester and Dryden." *RMS*, 5(1961):29–48.

10 RAMSEY, Paul. *The Art of John Dryden.* Lexington, Ky., 1969.

11 ROOT, Robert K. "Dryden's Conversion to the Roman Catholic Faith." *PMLA*, 20(1907):298–308.

12 ROPER, Alan H. "Dryden's 'Secular Masque.' " *MLQ*, 23(1962):29–40.

13 ROPER, Alan H. *Dryden's Poetic Kingdoms.* 1965.

14 SAINTSBURY, George. *Dryden.* (EML.) 1881.

15 SCHILLING, Bernard N., ed. *Dryden: A Collection of Critical Essays.* Englewood Cliffs, N.J., 1963.†

16 SCOTT, Walter. *Life of Dryden* [1834 text], ed. Bernard Kreissman. Lincoln, Neb., 1963.†

17 SIMON, Irène. "Dryden's Prose Style." *RLV*, 31(1965):506–30.

18 SMITH, David Nichol. *John Dryden.* (Clark Lectures, 1948–49.) Cambridge, 1950.

19 SMITH, John Harrington. "Some Sources of Dryden's Toryism, 1682–84." *HLQ*, 20(1957):233–43.

20 SÖDERLIND, Johannes. *Verb Syntax in John Dryden's Prose*, 2 vols. Uppsala, 1951, 1958.

21 SWEDENBERG, H. T., Jr. "Dryden's Obsessive Concern with the Heroic." *MacMillan Festschrift*, pp. 12–26.

22 SWEDENBERG, H. T., Jr., ed. *Essential Articles for the Study of John Dryden.* Hamden, Conn., 1966.

23 SWEDENBERG, H. T., Jr. "On Editing Dryden's Early Poems." *Campbell Festschrift*, pp. 73–84.

24 TURNELL, G. M. "Dryden and the Religious Elements in the Classical Tradition." *Englische Studien*, 70(1935):244–61.

25 VAN DOREN, Mark. *The Poetry of John Dryden.* New York, 1920. Repr. 1931.

26 VAN DOREN, Mark. *John Dryden: A Study of His Poetry.* New York, 1946.†

1 VERRALL, A. W. *Lectures on Dryden*. Cambridge, 1914.

2 WALLACE, John M. "Dryden and History: A Problem in Allegorical Reading." *ELH*, 36(1969):265–90.

3 WARD, Charles E. *The Life of John Dryden*. Chapel Hill, 1961.

4 WARD, Charles E., and H. T. SWEDENBERG. *John Dryden*. Los Angeles, 1967. [Papers read at a Clark Library Seminar. I: "Challenges to Dryden's Biographer." II: "Challenges to Dryden's Editor."]

5 WASSERMAN, George R. *John Dryden*. New York, 1964.

6 WELLE, J. A. van der. *Dryden and Holland*. Groningen, 1962.

7 YOUNG, Kenneth. *John Dryden: A Critical Biography*. 1954.

Absalom and Achitophel

8 BALL, Albert. "Charles II: Dryden's Christian Hero." *MP*, 59(1961):25–35.

9 BAUMGARTNER, A. M. "Dryden's Caleb and Agag." *RES*, n.s. 13(1962): 394–97.

10 BRODWIN, Leonora L. "Miltonic Allusion in *Absalom and Achitophel:* Its Function in the Political satire." *JEGP*, 68(1969):24–44.

11 CABLE, Chester H. " 'Absalom and Achitophel' as Epic Satire." *Studies in Honor of John Wilcox*. Detroit, 1958, pp. 51–60.

12 CHAMBERS, A. B. "*Absalom and Achitophel:* Christ and Satan." *MLN*, 74(1959):592–96.

13 DAVIES, Godfrey. "The Conclusion of Dryden's *Absalom and Achitophel*." *HLQ*, 10(1946):69–82.

14 DE BEER, E. S. "*Absalom and Achitophel:* Literary and Historical Notes." *RES*, 17(1941):298–309.

15 FERRY, Anne Davidson. *Milton and the Miltonic Dryden*. Cambridge, Mass., 1968. [Part 1: *Absalom and Achitophel*.]

16 FREEDMAN, Morris. "Dryden's Miniature Epic." *JEGP*, 57(1958):211–19.

17 FRENCH, A. L. "Dryden, Marvell and Political Poetry." *SEL*, 8(1968):397–413.

18 GUILHAMET, Leon M. "Dryden's Debasement of Scripture in *Abaslom and Achitophel*." *SEL*, 9(1969):395–413.

19 HAMMOND, H. " 'One Immortal Song.' " *RES*, n.s. 5(1954):60–62.

20 JONES, Harold W., ed. *Anti-Achitophel (1682): Three Verse Replies to "Absalom and Achitophel*." (*SF&R*.) Gainesville, Fla., 1961.

21 JONES, Richard F. "The Originality of *Absalom and Achitophel*." *MLN*, 46 (1931):211–18.

22 KING, Bruce. "*Absalom and Achitophel:* Machiavelli and the False Messiah." *EA*, 16(1963):250–54.

23 KING, Bruce. "Absalom and Dryden's Earlier Praise of Monmouth." *ES*, 46(1965):332–33.

1   KINNEAVY, Gerald B. "Judgment in Extremes: A Study of Dryden's *Absalom and Achitophel." University of Dayton Review*, 3 (1966):15–30.

2   KINSLEY, James. "Historical Allusions in *Absalom and Achitophel." RES*, n.s. 6(1955):291–7. [See also 7(1956):410–15.]

3   LEVINE, George R. "Dryden's 'Inarticulate Poesy': Music and the Davidic King in *Absalom and Achitophel." ECS*, 1(1968):291–312.

4   LEWALSKI, Barbara K. " 'David's Troubles Remembred': An Analogue to 'Absalom and Achitophel.' " *N&Q*, 209(1964):340–43.

5   LEWALSKI, Barbara K. "The Scope and Function of Biblical Allusion in *Absalom and Achitophel." ELN*, 3(1965):29–35.

6   McMANAWAY, James G. "Notes on 'A Key . . . to . . . Absalom and Achitophel.' " *N&Q*, 184(1943):365–66.

7   MAURER, Wallace. "The Immortalizing of Dryden's 'One Immortal Song.' " *N&Q*, 203(1958):341–43.

8   MAURER, Wallace. "Dryden's Balaam Well Hung?" *RES*, n.s. 10(1959): 398–401. [Sir Francis Winnington.]

9   MAURER, Wallace. "Who Prompted Dryden to Write *Absalom and Achitophel*?" *PQ*, 40(1961):130–38. [Edward Seymour.]

10 PETERSON, R. G. "Larger Manners and Events: Sallust and Virgil in *Absalom and Achitophel." PMLA*, 82(1967):236–44.

11 POLLOCK, John. *The Popish Plot: A Study in the History of the Reign of Charles II*. 1903.

12 RICKS, Christopher. "Dryden's Absalom." *EIC*, 11(1961):273–89.

13 SCHILLING, Bernard N. *Dryden and the Conservative Myth: A Reading of "Absalom and Achitophel."* New Haven, 1961.*

14 SCHLESS, Howard H. "Dryden's *Absalom and Achitophel* and *A Dialogue between Nathan and Absolome." PQ*, 40(1961):139–43.

15 WALLERSTEIN, Ruth. "To Madness Near Allied: Shaftesbury and His Place in the Design and Thought of *Absalom and Achitophel." HLQ*, 6(1943): 445–71.

16 WELLINGTON, James E. "Conflicting Concepts of Man in Dryden's *Absalom and Achitophel." Satire Newsletter*, 4(1966):2–11.

17 WOLF, J. Q. "A Note on Dryden's Zimri." *MLN*, 47(1932):97–99.

The Hind and the Panther

18 ANSELMENT, Raymond A. "Martin Marprelate: A New Source for Dryden's Fable of the Martin and the Swallows." *RES*, n.s. 17(1966):256–67.

19 BENSON, Donald R. "Theology and Politics in Dryden's Conversion." *SEL*, 4(1964):393–412.

1   HAMM, Victor M. "Dryden's *The Hind and the Panther* and Roman Catholic Apologetics." *PMLA*, 83(1968):400–415.

2   HOOKER, Helene Maxwell. "Charles Montagu's Reply to *The Hind and the Panther*." *ELH*, 8(1941):51–73.

3   KINSLEY, James. "Dryden's Bestiary." *RES*, n.s. 4(1953):331–36.

4   MILLER, Clarence H. "The Styles of *The Hind and the Panther*." *JEGP*, 61(1962):511–27.

5   MYERS, William. "Politics in *The Hind and the Panther*." *EIC*, 19(1969):19–34.

Mac Flecknoe

6   ALSSID, Michael W. "Shadwell's *Mac Flecknoe*." *SEL*, 7(1967):387–402.

7   BROOKS, Harold. "When Did Dryden Write *Mac Flecknoe?*—Some Additional Notes." *RES*, 11(1935):74–78.

8   DEARING, Vinton A. "Dryden's *Mac Flecknoe*: The Case for Authorial Revision." *SB*, 7(1955):85–102.

9   ELLIS, Amanda M. "Horace's Influence on Dryden." *PQ*, 4(1925):39–60.

10 EVANS, G. Blakemore. "The Text of Dryden's *Mac Flecknoe*." *HLB*, 7(1953):32–54.

11 EVANS, G. Blakemore. "Dryden's *Mac Flecknoe* and Dekker's *Satiromastix*." *MLN*, 76(1961):598–600.

12 KORN, A. L. "*Mac Flecknoe* and Cowley's *Davideis*." *HLQ*, 14(1951):99–127.

13 McFADDEN, George. "Elkanah Settle and the Genesis of *Mac Flecknoe*." *PQ*, 43(1964):55–72.

14 McKEITHAN, Daniel M. "The Occasion of *Mac Flecknoe*." *PMLA*, 47(1932):766–71.

15 SMITH, R. Jack. "The Date of *Mac Flecknoe*." *RES*, 18(1942):322–23.

16 TANNER, J. E. "The Messianic Image in *Mac Flecknoe*." *MLN*, 76(1961):220–23.

17 TAYLOR, Aline M. "Dryden's 'Enchanted Isle' and Shadwell's 'Dominion.'" *MacMillan Festschrift*. Chapel Hill, 1967, pp. 39–53.

18 THORN-DRURY, G. "Dryden's '*Mac Flecknoe*': A Vindication." *MLR*, 13(1918):276–81.

19 TOWERS, Tom H. "The Lineage of Shadwell: An Approach to *Mac Flecknoe*." *SEL*, 3(1963):323–34.

Religio Laici

1 BENSON, Donald R. "Who 'Bred' *Religio Laici?*" *JEGP*, 65(1966):238–51.

2 BROWN, David D. "Dryden's 'Religio Laici' and the 'Judicious and Learned Friend.' " *MLR*, 56(1961):66–69. [Tillotson.]

3 CHIASSON, Elias J. "Dryden's Apparent Scepticism in *Religio Laici.*" *Harvard Theological Review*, 54 (1961):207–21.

4 CORDER, Jim W. "Rhetoric and Meaning in *Religio Laici.*" *PMLA*, 82(1967):245–49.

5 FUJIMURA, Thomas H. "Dryden's *Religio Laici:* An Anglican Poem." *PMLA*, 76(1961):205–17.

6 HAMM, Victor M. "Dryden's *Religio Laici* and Roman Catholic Apologetics." *PMLA*, 80(1965):190–98.

7 HOOKER, Edward N. "Dryden and the Atoms of Epicurus." *ELH*, 24(1957):177–90.

8 WARD, C. E. " 'Religio Laici' and Father Simon's 'History.' " *MLN*, 61(1946):407–12.

9 WELCHER, Jeanne K. "The Opening of *Religio Laici* and Its Virgilian Associations." *SEL*, 8(1968):391–96.

Other Poems

10 BRENNECKE, Ernest. "Dryden's Odes to Draghi's Music." *PMLA*, 49(1934):1–36.

11 FOWLER, Alastair, and Douglas BROOKS. "The Structure of Dryden's 'Song for St. Cecilia's Day, 1687.' " *EIC*, 17(1967):434–47.

12 FOXELL, Nigel. *Ten Poems Analyzed.* Oxford, 1966. [*Alexander's Feast.*]

13 HINNANT, Charles H. "Dryden's Gallic Rooster." *SP*, 65(1968):647–56. [*The Cock and the Fox.*]

14 HOLLANDER, John. *The Untuning of the Sky.* Princeton, 1961. [Pp. 401–22: "The Odes to Music."]

15 HOOKER, Edward N. "The Purpose of Dryden's *Annus Mirabilis.*" *HLQ*, 10(1946):49–67.

16 HOPE, A. D. "Anne Killigrew or the Art of Modulating." *SoRA*, 1(1963):4–14.

17 JOOST, Nicholas. "Dryden's *Medal* and the Baroque in Politics and the Arts." *Modern Age*, 3(1959):148–55.

18 KINSLEY, James. "The 'Three Glorious Victories' in *Annus Mirabilis.*" *RES*, n.s. 7(1956):29–37.

19 LEGOUIS, Pierre. "Dryden's Scipio and Hannibal." *TLS*, July 15, 1965, p. 602. [*The Medall*].

20 LEVINE, Jay Arnold. "John Dryden's Epistle to John Driden." *JEGP*, 63 (1964):450–74.

1 LEVINE, Jay Arnold. "Dryden's *Song for St. Cecilia's Day, 1687.*" *PQ*, 44(1965):38–50.

2 MACE, D. T. "Musical Humanism, the Doctrine of Rhythmus, and the Saint Cecilia Odes of Dryden." *JWCI*, 27(1964):251–92.

3 MARY ELEANOR, Mother. "*Anne Killigrew* and *Mac Flecknoe.*" *PQ*, 43(1964):47–54.

4 MAURER, A. E. Wallace. "The Design of Dryden's *The Medall.*" *PLL*, 2 (1966):293–304.

5 MAURER, A. E. Wallace. "The Structure of Dryden's *Astraea Redux.*" *PLL*, 2(1966):13–20.

6 PETERSON, R. G. "The Unavailing Gift: Dryden's Roman Farewell to Mr. Oldham." *MP*, 66(1969):232–36.

7 ROPER, Alan H. "Dryden's *Medal* and the Divine Analogy." *ELH*, 29(1962): 396–417.

8 ROSENBERG, Bruce A. "*Annus Mirabilis* Distilled." *PMLA*, 79(1964): 254–58. [Alchemical and astrological allusions.]

9 SMITH, John Harrington. "Dryden's Prologue and Epilogue to *Mithridates*, Revived." *PMLA*, 68(1953):251–67.

10 STEADMAN, John M. "Timotheus in Dryden, E. K., and Gafori." *TLS*, Dec. 16, 1960, p. 819.

11 SUTHERLAND, W. O. S., Jr. "Dryden's Use of Popular Imagery in *The Medal.*" *University of Texas Studies in English*, 35(1956):123–34.

12 SWEDENBERG, H. T., Jr. "England's Joy: *Astraea Redux* in its Setting." *SP*, 50(1953):30–44.

13 TILLYARD, E. M. W. *Five Poems.* 1948. [Pp. 49–65: *Ode to Anne Killigrew.*]

14 VIETH, David M. "Irony in Dryden's *Ode to Anne Killigrew.*" *SP*, 62(1965): 91–100.

15 WALLERSTEIN, Ruth. " 'On the Death of Mrs. Killigrew': The Perfecting of a Genre." *SP*, 44(1947):519–28.

16 WASSERMAN, Earl R. "The Meaning of 'Poland' in *The Medal.*" *MLN*, 73(1958):165–67.

17 WASSERMAN, Earl R. *The Subtler Language.* Baltimore, 1959. [Chap. ii: "Dryden: Epistle to Charleton."]

18 WRIGHT, Herbert G. "Some Sidelights on the Reputation and Influence of Dryden's *Fables.*" *RES*, 21(1945):23–37.

Plays

19 ALLEN, Ned Bliss. *The Sources of John Dryden's Comedies.* Ann Arbor, 1935.

20 BLEULER, Werner. *Das heroische Drama John Drydens als Experiment dekorativer Formkunst.* Bern, 1958.

21 BOWERS, Fredson T. "Variants in Early Editions of Dryden's Plays." *HLB*, 3(1949):278–88.

22 FUJIMURA, Thomas H. "The Appeal of Dryden's Heroic Plays." *PMLA*, 75(1960):37–45.

1 GAGEN, Jean. "Love and Honor in Dryden's Heroic Plays." *PMLA*, 77(1962):208–20.

2 HARTSOCK, Mildred E. "Dryden's Plays: A Study in Ideas." *Seventeenth-Century Studies, Second Series, by Members of the Graduate School, University of Cincinnati*, ed. Robert Shafer. Princeton, 1937, pp. 71–176.

3 JEFFERSON, D. W. "The Significance of Dryden's Heroic Plays." *PLPLS-LHS*, 5(1940):125–39.

4 JEFFERSON, D. W. " 'All, All of a Piece Throughout': Thoughts on Dryden's Dramatic Poetry." *Restoration Theatre*, ed. John Russell Brown and Bernard Harris (Stratford-upon-Avon Studies, 6). London and New York, 1965, pp. 159–76.

5 KING, Bruce. *Dryden's Major Plays*. Edinburgh, 1966; New York, 1967.

6 KIRSCH, Arthur C. *Dryden's Heroic Drama*. Princeton, 1965.

7 LOFTIS, John. "The Hispanic Element in Dryden." *Emory University Quarterly*, 20(1964):90–100.

8 MOORE, Frank Harper. *The Nobler Pleasure: Dryden's Comedy in Theory and Practice*. Chapel Hill, 1963.

9 MOORE, John Robert. "Political Allusions in Dryden's Later Plays." *PMLA*, 73(1958):36–42.

10 OSBORN, Scott C. "Heroical Love in Dryden's Heroic Drama." *PMLA*, 73(1958):480–90.

11 PENDLEBURY, B. J. *Dryden's Heroic Plays: A Study of the Origins*. 1923.

12 RUSSELL, Trusten W. *Voltaire, Dryden, and Heroic Tragedy*. New York, 1946.

13 WAITH, Eugene M. *The Herculean Hero in Marlowe, Chapman, Shakespeare, and Dryden*. New York and London, 1962.

14 WAITH, Eugene M. "The Voice of Mr. Bayes." *SEL*, 3(1963):335–43. [The dedications to the plays.]

15 WINTERBOTTOM, John A. "The Development of the Hero in Dryden's Tragedies." *JEGP*, 52(1953):161–73.

16 WINTERBOTTOM, John A. "The Place of Hobbesian Ideas in Dryden's Tragedies." *JEGP*, 57(1958):665–83.

17 WINTERBOTTOM, John A. "Stoicism in Dryden's Tragedies." *JEGP*, 61 (1962):868–83.

18 ZEBOUNI, Selma. *Dryden: A Study in Heroic Characterization*. Baton Rouge, 1965.

ALL FOR LOVE, OR THE WORLD WELL LOST

Editions: John J. Enck, New York, 1966(†); Ben Griffith, Woodbury, New York, 1960; R. J. Kaufmann, San Francisco, 1962(†); with *The Spanish Friar*, W. Strunk, Boston, 1911. [*All for Love* is included in most anthologies of Restoration and eighteenth-century plays.]

1 CORACCIOLO, Peter. "Dryden and the 'Antony and Cleopatra' of Sir Charles Sedley." *ES, Anglo-American Supplement*, 1969, pp. l–lv.

2 DAVIES, H. Neville. "Dryden's 'All for Love' and Thomas May's 'The Tragedie of Cleopatra Queen of Aegypt.' " *N&Q*, 210 (1965), 139–44.

3 DAVIES, H. Neville. "Dryden's 'All for Love' and Sedley's 'Antony and Cleopatra.' " *N&Q*, 212(1967):221–27.

4 DOBRÉE, Bonamy. "Cleopatra and 'That Criticall Warr.' " *TLS*, Oct. 11, 1928, pp. 717–18.

5 FERRY, Anne Davidson. *Milton and the Miltonic Dryden*. Cambridge, Mass., 1968. [Part 2: *Samson Agonistes* and *All for Love*.]

6 GOGGIN, L. P. "This Bow of Ulysses." *Essays and Studies in Language and Literature*. Pittsburgh, 1964, pp. 49–86.

7 JACKSON, Wallace. "Dryden's Emperor and Lillo's Merchant: The Relevant Bases of Action." *MLQ*, 26(1965):536–44.

8 KING, Bruce. "Dryden's Intent in *All for Love*." *College English*, 24(1963): 267–71.

9 KING, Bruce, ed. *Twentieth-Century Interpretations of "All for Love."* Englewood Cliffs, N.J., 1968.

10 LEAVIS, F. R. " 'Antony and Cleopatra' and 'All for Love.' " *Scrutiny*, 5(1936):158–69.

11 MUIR, Kenneth. "The Imagery of *All for Love*." *PLPLS-LHS*, 5(1940):140–47.

12 NAZARETH, Peter. "*All for Love:* Dryden's Hybrid Play." *ESA*, 6(1963): 154–63.

13 REINERT, Otto. "Passion and Pity in *All for Love:* A Reconsideration." *The Hidden Sense and Other Essays* by Maren-Sofie Røstvig and others. Oslo and New York, 1963, pp. 159–95.

14 STARNES, D. T. "Imitation of Shakespeare in Dryden's *All for Love*." *TSLL*, 6(1964):39–46.

15 SUCKLING, Norman. "Dryden in Egypt: Reflexions on *All for Love*." *DUJ*, 45(1952):2–7.

16 WEINBROT, Howard D. "Alexas in *All for Love:* His Genealogy and Function." *SP*, 64(1967):625–39.

AMBOYNA

17 BREDVOLD, Louis I. "Political Aspects of Dryden's *Amboyna* and *The Spanish Fryar*." *UMSLL*, 8(1932):119–32.

THE ASSIGNATION, OR LOVE IN A NUNNERY

18 MOORE, Frank H. "Heroic Comedy: A New Interpretation of Dryden's *Assignation*." *SP*, 51(1954):585–98.

19 RUNDLE, James U. "The Sources of Dryden's 'Comic Plot' in *The Assignation*." *MP*, 45(1947):104–11. [Calderón.]

AURENG-ZEBE

1 ALSSID, Michael W. "The Design of Dryden's *Aureng-Zebe.*" *JEGP,* 64(1965):452–69.

DON SEBASTIAN, KING OF PORTUGAL

2 KING, Bruce. "*Don Sebastian:* Dryden's Moral Fable." *Sewanee Review,* 70(1962):651–70.

AN EVENING'S LOVE, OR THE MOCK ASTROLOGER

3 ALLEN, Ned B. "The Sources of Dryden's *The Mock Astrologer.*" *PQ,* 36(1957):453–64.

THE INDIAN EMPEROUR

4 ALSSID, Michael W. "The Perfect Conquest: A Study of Theme, Structure and Characters in Dryden's *The Indian Emperor.*" *SP,* 59(1962):539–59.
5 BOWERS, Fredson T. "Current Theories of Copy-Text, with an Illustration from Dryden." *MP,* 68(1950):12–20.
6 BOWERS, Fredson T. "The 1665 Manuscript of Dryden's *Indian Emperour.*" *SP,* 48(1951):738–60.
7 LOFTIS, John. "Exploration and Enlightenment: Dryden's *The Indian Emperour* and Its Background." *PQ,* 45(1966):71–84.
8 MacMILLAN, Dougald. "The Sources of Dryden's *The Indian Emperour.*" *HLQ,* 13(1950):355–70.
9 PERKINS, Merle L. "Dryden's *The Indian Emperour* and Voltaire's *Alzire.*" *CL,* 9(1957):229–37.
10 RINGLER, Richard N. "Two Sources for Dryden's *The Indian Emperour.*" *PQ,* 42(1963):423–29. [Donne and Spenser.]
11 SHERGOLD, N. D., and Peter URE. "Dryden and Calderón: A New Spanish Source for 'The Indian Emperour.' " *MLR,* 61(1966):369–83.
12 STECK, James S. "Dryden's *Indian Emperour:* The Early Editions and Their Relation to the Text." *SB,* 2(1949–50):139–52.

THE INDIAN QUEEN

13 SMITH, John Harrington. "The Dryden-Howard Collaboration." *SP,* 51(1954):54–74.

MARRIAGE À LA MODE

14 KING, Bruce. "Dryden's *Marriage à la Mode.*" *DramS,* 4(1965):28–37.

SIR MARTIN MAR-ALL

1 MOORE, F. H. "The Composition of *Sir Martin Mar-All*." *MacMillan Festschrift*, pp. 27–38.

THE SPANISH FRYAR
Edition: [with *All for Love*] W. Strunk, Boston, 1911.

2 BREDVOLD, Louis I. "Political Aspects of Dryden's *Amboyna* and *The Spanish Fryar*." *UMSLL*, 8 (1932), 119–32.
3 LEGOUIS, Pierre. "Quinault et Dryden: Une source de *The Spanish Fryar*." *RLC*, 11(1931):398–415.

THE STATE OF INNOCENCE, AND FALL OF MAN

4 BOWERS, Fredson. "The Pirated Quarto of Dryden's *State of Innocence*." *SB*, 5(1952–53):166–69.
5 HAMILTON, Marion H. "The Early Editions of Dryden's *State of Innocence*." *SB*, 5(1952–53):163–66.
6 HAMILTON, Marion H. "The Manuscripts of Dryden's *The State of Innocence* and the Relation of the Harvard MS to the First Quarto." *SB*, 6(1954):237–46.
7 KING, Bruce. "The Significance of Dryden's *State of Innocence*." *SEL*, 4(1964):371–91.
8 McFADDEN, George. "Dryden's 'Most Barren Period'—and Milton." *HLQ*, 24(1961):283–96.

TYRANNICK LOVE, OR THE ROYAL MARTYR

9 ADAMS, Henry H. "A Prompt Copy of Dryden's *Tyrannic Love*." *SB*, 4(1951–52):170–74.
10 KING, Bruce. "Dryden, Tillotson, and *Tyrannic Love*." *RES*, n.s. 16(1965):364–77.

THE WILD GALLANT

11 BOWERS, Fredson T. "The First Edition of Dryden's *Wild Gallant*." *The Library*, 5th ser., 5(1950):51–54.

Critical Writings

12 *Essays*, ed. W. P. Ker. 2 vols. Oxford, 1900.
13 *Of Dramatic Poesy and Other Critical Essays*, ed. George Watson. (EL.) 2 vols. 1962.*

1 *An Essay of Dramatic Poesy (and Other Essays)*, ed. John L. Mahoney. Indianapolis, 1965.†

2 *Literary Criticism of John Dryden*, ed. Arthur C. Kirsch. (Regents Critics Series.) Lincoln, Neb., 1966.

3 ADEN, John M. *The Critical Opinions of John Dryden: A Dictionary.* Nashville, 1963.

4 ADEN, John M. "Dryden and Boileau: The Question of Critical Influence. *SP*, 50(1953):491–509.

5 ADEN, John M. "Dryden, Corneille, and the *Essay of Dramatic Poesy*." *RES*, n.s. 6(1955):147–56.

6 ADEN, John M. "Dryden and the Imagination: The First Phase." *PMLA*, 74(1959):28–40.

7 ARCHER, Stanley. "The Persons in *An Essay of Dramatic Poesy*." *PLL*, 2(1966):305–14.

8 BATELY, Janet M. "Dryden's Revisions in the *Essay of Dramatic Poesy:* The Preposition at the End of the Sentence and the Expression of the Relative." *RES*, n.s. 15(1964):268–82.

9 BOHN, William E. "The Development of John Dryden's Literary Criticism." *PMLA*, 22(1907):56–139.

10 BOTTKOL, J. McG. "Dryden's Latin Scholarship." *MP*, 40(1943):241–54.

11 BROWN, David D. "John Tillotson's Revisions and Dryden's 'Talent for English Prose.'" *RES*, n.s. 12(1961):24–39.

12 DOYLE, Anne. "Dryden's Authorship of *Notes and Observations on The Empress of Morocco* (1674)." *SEL*, 6(1966):421–45.

13 EIDSON, J. O. "Dryden's Criticism of Shakespeare." *SP*, 33(1936):273–80.

14 ELLIS, Amanda M. "Horace's Influence on Dryden." *PQ*, 4(1925):39–60.

15 FEDER, Lillian. "John Dryden's Use of Classical Rhetoric." *PMLA*, 69 (1954):1258–78.

16 FREEDMAN, Morris. "Milton and Dryden on Rhyme." *HLQ*, 24(1961): 337–44.

17 GATTO, Louis C. "An Annotated Bibliography of Critical Thought Concerning Dryden's *Essay of Dramatic Poesy*." *RECTR*, 5(1966):18–29.

18 HATHAWAY, Baxter. "John Dryden and the Function of Tragedy." *PMLA*, 58(1943):665–73.

19 HUME, Robert D. "Dryden's 'Heads of an Answer to Rymer': Notes toward a Hypothetical Revolution." *RES*, n.s. 19(1968):373–86.

20 HUNTLEY, Frank L. "Dryden's Discovery of Boileau." *MP*, 45(1947): 112–17.

1 HUNTLEY, Frank L. *On Dryden's "Essay of Dramatic Poesy."* Ann Arbor, 1951.

2 JAMESON, R. D. "Notes on Dryden's Lost Prosodia." *MP*, 20(1923):241–53.

3 JENSEN, H. James. *A Glossary of John Dryden's Critical Terms.* Minneapolis, 1969.

7 LEGOUIS, Pierre. "Corneille and Dryden as Dramatic Critics." *Seventeenth Century Studies Presented to Sir Herbert Grierson.* Oxford, 1938, pp. 269–91.

5 LOWENS, Irving. "St. Evremond, Dryden, and the Theory of Opera." *Criticism*, 1(1959):226–48.

6 MACE, Dean T. "Dryden's Dialogue on Drama." *JWCI*, 25(1962):87–112.

7 McFADDEN, George. "Dryden, Boileau, and Longinian Imitation." *Proc. Fourth International Comparative Literary Association of Fribourg.* The Hague, 2(1966):751–55.

8 MONK, Samuel H. "Dryden and the Beginnings of Shakespeare Criticism in the Augustan Age." *The Persistence of Shakespeare Idolatry: Essays in Honor of Robert W. Babcock.* Detroit, 1964, pp. 47–75.

9 MURPHREE, A. A. "Wit and Dryden." *All These to Teach: Essays in Honor of C. A. Robertson.* Gainesville, Fla., 1965, pp. 159–70.

10 NÄNNY, Max. *John Drydens Rhetorische Poetik: Versuch eines Aufbaus aus seinem kritischen Schaffen.* Bern, 1959.

11 RUDD, Niall. "Dryden on Horace and Juvenal." *UTQ*, 32 (1963), 155–69.

12 SHERWOOD, John C. "Dryden and the Rules: The Preface to *Troilus and Cressida*," *CL*, 2(1950):73–83.

13 SHERWOOD, John C. "Dryden and the Critical Theories of Tasso." *CL*, 18(1966):351–59.

14 SHERWOOD, John C. "Precept and Practice in Dryden's Criticism." *JEGP*, 68(1969):432–40.

15 SINGH, Sarup. "Dryden and the Unities." *IJES*, 2(1961):78–90.

16 SMITH, John Harrington. "Dryden and the Rules: The Preface to the *Fables*." *JEGP*, 52(1953):12–26.

17 STRANG, Barbara M. H. "Dryden's Innovations in Critical Vocabulary." *DUJ*, 51(1959):114–23.

18 THALE, Mary. "Dryden's Critical Vocabulary: The Imitation of Nature." *PLL*, 2(1966):315–26.

19 THALE, Mary. "Dryden's Dramatic Criticism: Polestar of the Ancients." *CL*, 18(1966):36–54.

20 TILLYARD, E. M. W. "A Note on Dryden's Criticism." *Jones Festschrift*, pp. 330–38.

21 TROWBRIDGE, Hoyt. "Dryden's *Essay on the Dramatic Poetry of the Last Age*." *PQ*, 22(1943):240–50.

22 TROWBRIDGE, Hoyt. "The Place of Rules in Dryden's Criticism." *MP*, 44(1946):84–96.

1 WALCOTT, F. G. "John Dryden's Answer to Thomas Rymer's *The Tragedies of the Last Age.*" *PQ*, 15(1936):194–214.

2 WALLERSTEIN, Ruth. "Dryden and the Analysis of Shakespeare's Techniques." *RES*, 19(1943):165–85.

3 WATSON, George. "Dryden's First Answer to Rymer." *RES*, n.s. 14(1963): 17–23.

4 WILLIAMSON, George. "The Occasion of *An Essay of Dramatic Poesy.*" *MP*, 44(1946):1–9.

5 WILLIAMSON, George. *Milton and Others.* Chicago, 1965. [Pp. 103–21: "Dryden's View of Milton."]

Translations

6 *The Works of Virgil, translated by John Dryden.* With Introduction by James Kinsley. 1961.

7 BARNARD, John. "Dryden, Tonson, and Subscriptions for the 1697 *Virgil.*" *PBSA*, 57(1963):129–51.

8 BOTTKOL, J. McG. "Dryden's Latin Scholarship." *MP*, 40(1943):241–54.

9 FROST, William. *Dryden and the Art of Translation.* New Haven, 1955.

10 GALLAGHER, Mary. "Dryden's Translation of Lucretius." *HLQ*, 28(1964): 19–29.

11 HOOKER, Helene M. "Dryden's *Georgics* and English Predecessors." *HLQ*, 9(1946):273–310.

12 MINER, Earl. "Dryden's Messianic Eclogue." *RES*, n.s. 11(1960):299–302. [The translation of Virgil's Fourth Eclogue.]

13 PROUDFOOT, L. *Dryden's "Aeneid" and its Seventeenth-Century Predecessors.* Manchester and New York, 1960.

Poetry

Bibliography

14 ALDEN, John. *The Muses Mourn: A Checklist of Verse Occasioned by the Death of Charles II.* Charlottesville, Va., 1958.

15 CASE, Arthur E. *A Bibliography of English Poetical Miscellanies, 1521–1750.* Oxford, 1935.

1   DAY, Cyrus L., and Eleanore B. MURRIE. *English Song-Books, 1651–1702: A Bibliography, with a First-Line Index of Songs.* 1940.

2   LEACH, Elsie. "English Religious Poetry, 1600–1699: A Partial Bibliography." *Bulletin of Bibliography*, 23(1961):132–35.

3   OSBORNE, Mary T. *Advice-to-a-Painter Poems, 1633–1856: An Annotated Finding List.* Austin, 1949.

4   PINTO, V. de Sola. *The Restoration Court Poets.* (*WTW.*) 1965.

Collections

5   DANIELSSON, Bror, and David M. VIETH, eds. *Collection of English Poetry Principally Political and Satyrs from the Last Years of Charles II.* Stockholm, 1967.

6   LOVE, Harold, ed. *The Penguin Book of Restoration Verse.* 1968.

7   PINTO, Vivian de Sola, ed. *Poetry of the Restoration, 1653–1700.* New York, 1966.

8   *Poems on Affairs of State: Augustan Satirical Verse, 1660–1714.* New Haven, 1963. Vol. I: *1660–1678*, ed. George de F. Lord (1963). Vol. II: *1678–1681*, ed. Elias F. Mengel, Jr. (1965). Vol. III: *1682–1685*, ed. Howard H. Schless (1967). Vol. IV: *1685–1688*, ed. Galbraith M. Crump (1968).

General Studies

9   BALLIET, Conrad A. "The History and Rhetoric of the Triplet." *PMLA*, 80(1965):528–34.

10 BEVAN, Allan. "Poetry and Politics in Restoration England." *Dalhousie Review*, 39(1959):314–25.

11 BOYS, Richard C. "Some Problems of Dryden's Miscellany." *ELH*, 7(1940):130–43.

12 BROOKS, Harold F. "The 'Imitation' in English Poetry, Especially in Formal Satire, before the Age of Pope." *RES*, 25(1949):124–40.

13 CHERNAIK, Warren L. "The Heroic Occasional Poem: Panegyric and Satire in the Restoration." *MLQ*, 26(1965):523–35.

14 CONGLETON, James E. "The Effect of the Restoration on Poetry." *TSL*, 6(1961):93–101.

15 GOLDGAR, Bertrand A. "Satires on Man and 'The Dignity of Human Nature.'" *PMLA*, 80(1965):535–41.

16 HAGSTRUM, Jean H. *The Sister Arts: The Tradition of Literary Pictorialism and English Poetry from Dryden to Gray.* Chicago, 1958.

17 HAMILTON, K[enneth] G. *The Two Harmonies: Poetry and Prose in the Seventeenth Century.* Oxford, 1963.

18 HAYMAN, John. "Raillery in Restoration Satire." *HLQ*, 31(1968):107–22.

1 HOLLANDER, John. *The Untuning of the Sky: Ideas of Music in English Poetry, 1500–1700*. Princeton, 1961.

2 JACK, Ian. *Augustan Satire: Intention and Idiom in English Poetry, 1660–1750*. Oxford, 1952.†

3 KITCHIN, George. *A Survey of Burlesque and Parody in English*. Edinburgh, 1931.

4 MACDONALD, Hugh. "Some Poetical Miscellanies, 1672–1716." *E&S*, 26(1940):106–12.

5 NEVO, Ruth. *The Dial of Virtue: A Study of Poems on Affairs of State in the Seventeenth Century*. Princeton, 1963.

6 NICOLSON, Marjorie H. *The Breaking of the Circle: Studies in the Effect of the "New Science" upon Seventeenth-Century Poetry*. Evanston, 1950. Rev. ed., New York, 1960.†

7 PELTZ, Catharine W. "The Neo-Classic Lyric, 1660–1725." *ELH*, 11(1944):92–116.

8 QUAINTANCE, Richard E. "French Sources of the Restoration 'Imperfect Enjoyment' Poem." *PQ*, 42(1963):190–99.

9 ROBERTS, William. "Saint-Amant, Orinda and Dryden's Miscellany." *ELN*, 1(1964):191–96.

10 SHARROCK, Roger. "Modes of Satire." *Restoration Theatre*, ed. John Russell Brown and Bernard Harris. (Stratford-upon-Avon Studies, 6.) London and New York, 1965, pp. 109–32.

11 WALLERSTEIN, Ruth C. "The Development of the Rhetoric and Metre of the Heroic Couplet, especially in 1625–1645." *PMLA*, 50(1935):166–209.

12 WASSERMAN, Earl R. "Pre-Restoration Poetry in Dryden's Miscellany." *MLN*, 52(1937):545–55.

13 WEINBROT, Howard D. "The Pattern of Formal Verse Satire in the Restoration and the Eighteenth Century." *PMLA*, 80(1965):394–401.

14 WEST, Albert H. *L'Influence française dans la poésie burlesque en Angleterre entre 1660 et 1700*. 1931.

15 WILLIAMSON, George. "The Rhetorical Pattern of Neo-Classical Wit." *MP*, 33(1935):55–81. Repr. in *Seventeenth-Century Contexts*, 1960, pp. 240–71.

16 WILSON, John Harold. *The Court Wits of the Restoration: An Introduction*. Princeton, 1948. Repr. 1968.

17 WOOD, Henry. "Beginnings of the 'Classical' Heroic Couplet in England." *American Journal of Philology*, 11(1890):55–79.

Butler, Samuel (*1613–1680*)

18 *Characters*, ed. Charles W. Daves. Cleveland, 1969.

19 *Collected Works*, ed. A. R. Waller (Vols. I, II) and René Lamar (Vol. III). 3 vols. Cambridge, 1905, 1908, 1928.

20 *Hudibras*, ed. John Wilders. Oxford, 1967.

1 *Three Poems*, ed. Alexander C. Spence. (ARS, 88.) Los Angeles, 1961. ("To the Memory of . . . Du-Vall," "Satyr on our Ridiculous Imitation of the French," and "The Elephant in the Moon.")

2 BAUER, Josephine. "Some Verse Fragments and Prose *Characters* by Samuel Butler not included in the *Complete Works.*" *MP*, 45(1948):160–68.

3 BENTLEY, Norma. "Another Butler Manuscript." *MP*, 46(1948):132–35.

4 BENTLEY, Norma. " 'Hudibras' Butler Abroad," *MLN*, 60(1945):254–59.

5 CURTISS, Joseph T. "Butler's *Sidrophel.*" *PMLA*, 44(1929):1066–78.

6 DE BEER, E. S. "The Later Life of Samuel Butler." *RES*, 4(1928):159–66.

7 GIBSON, Dan. "Samuel Butler." *Seventeenth-Century Studies by Members of the Graduate School, University of Cincinnati*, ed. Robert Shafer. Princeton, 1933, pp. 279–335.

8 LAMAR, René. "Du nouveau sur l'auteur d' 'Hudibras': Samuel Butler en Worcestershire." *RAA*, 1(1924):213–27.

9 LAMAR, René. "Samuel Butler à l'École du Roi." *EA*, 5(1952):17–24.

10 LAMAR, René. "Samuel Butler et la justice de son temps." *EA*, 7(1954): 271–79.

11 LEYBURN, Ellen. "*Hudibras* considered as Satiric Allegory." *HLQ*, 16 (1953):141–60.

12 MILLER, Ward S. "The Allegory in Part I of *Hudibras.*" *HLQ*, 21(1958): 323–43.

13 QUINTANA, Ricardo. "The Butler-Oxenden Correspondence." *MLN*, 48(1933):1–11, 486.

14 QUINTANA, Ricardo. "Samuel Butler: A Restoration Figure in a Modern Light." *ELH*, 18(1951):7–13.

15 RICHARDS, Edward A. *Hudibras in the Burlesque Tradition.* New York, 1937.

16 THORSON, James L. "The Publication of *Hudibras.*" *PBSA*, 60(1966): 418–38.

17 VELDKAMP, Jan. *Samuel Butler, the Author of Hudibras.* Hilversum, Netherlands, 1923.

Cotton, Charles (1630–1687)

18 *Poems*, ed. John Beresford. 1923.

19 *Poems*, ed. John Buxton. (Muses' Library.) London and Cambridge, Mass., 1958.

1 EVANS, Willa M. "Henry Lawes and Charles Cotton." *PMLA*, 53(1938): 724–29.

2 HUSSEY, Richard. "The Text of Cotton's Poems." *N&Q*, 186(1944):87–88.

3 SEMBOWER, Charles J. *The Life and the Poetry of Charles Cotton*. Philadelphia and New York, 1911.

Dorset, Charles Sackville, Earl of (1638–1706)

BIBLIOGRAPHY

4 BAGLEY, Helen A. "A Checklist of the Poems of Charles Sackville, Sixth Earl of Dorset and Middlesex." *MLN*, 47(1932):454–61.

5 HARRIS, Brice. *Charles Sackville, Sixth Earl of Dorset, Patron and Poet of the Restoration*. Urbana, 1940.

6 HOWARTH, R. G. "Some Additions to the Poems of Lord Dorset." *MLN*, 50(1935):457–59.

7 LEGOUIS, Pierre. "The Original of Dorset's Lampoon on Madame de Maintenon." *MLR*, 54(1959):66–68.

Halifax, Charles Montagu, Earl of (1661–1715)

8 HOOKER, Helene Maxwell. "Charles Montagu's Reply to *The Hind and the Panther*." *ELH*, 8(1941):51–73.

9 KERR, John D. "An Unpublished Manuscript of Charles Montagu, Earl of Halifax (1661–1715)." *JEGP*, 32(1933):66–69.

Mulgrave, John Sheffield, Earl of (1648–1721) (afterward Marquis of Normanby and Duke of Buckinghamshire)

10 IRVINE, Maurice. "Identification of Characters in Mulgrave's 'Essay upon Satyr.'" *SP*, 34(1937):533–51.

Oldham, John (1653–1683)

1 *Poems*, with an Introduction by Bonamy Dobrée. (Centaur Classics.) London and Carbondale, Ill., 1960.

BIBLIOGRAPHY

2 BROOKS, Harold F. "A Bibliography of John Oldham, the Restoration Satirist." *Proceedings and Papers of the Oxford Bibliographical Society*, 5(1936):1–38.

3 CABLE, Chester H. "Oldham's Borrowings from Buchanan." *MLN*, 66 (1951):523–27.

4 MACKIN, Cooper R. "The Satiric Technique of John Oldham's *Satyrs upon the Jesuits*." *SP*, 62(1965):78–90.

5 WILLIAMS, Weldon M. "The Genesis of John Oldham's *Satyrs upon the Jesuits*." *PMLA*, 58(1943):958–70.

6 WILLIAMS, Weldon M. "The Influence of Ben Jonson's *Catiline* upon John Oldham's *Satyrs upon the Jesuits*." *ELH*, 11(1944):38–62.

Philips, Katherine (1632–1664)

7 GOSSE, Edmund. *Seventeenth Century Studies*. 1883. [Pp. 203–30: "The Matchless Orinda."]

8 ROBERTS, William. "Saint-Amant, Orinda and Dryden's Miscellany." *ELN*, 1(1964):191–96.

9 SOUERS, Philip W. *The Matchless Orinda*. Cambridge, Mass., 1931.

Rochester, John Wilmot, Earl of (1647–1680)

10 *Collected Works*, ed. John Hayward. 1926.

11 *Complete Poems*, ed. David M. Vieth. New Haven, 1968.

12 *The Famous Pathologist, or The Noble Mountebank* [by Rochester and Thomas Alcock], ed. V. de Sola Pinto. Nottingham, 1961.

13 *Rochester's Poems on Several Occasions*, ed. James Thorpe. Princeton, 1950.

14 *Poems*, ed. Vivian de Sola Pinto. (Muses' Library.) London and Cambridge, Mass., 1953. 2nd ed., 1964.

15 *The Rochester-Savile Letters, 1671–1680*, ed. John H. Wilson. Columbus, Ohio, 1941.

1   AUFFRET, Jean. "Rochester's *Farewell.*" *EA*, 12(1959):142-50.

2   BERMAN, Ronald. "Rochester and the Defeat of the Senses." *Kenyon Review*, 26(1964):354-68.

3   BRUSER, Fredelle. "Disproportion: A Study in the Work of John Wilmot, Earl of Rochester." *UTQ*, 15 (1946):384-96.

4   CROCKER, S. F. "Rochester's *Satire against Mankind:* A Study of Certain Aspects of the Background." (West Virginia University Studies, 3.) 1937, 57-73.

5   ERSKINE-HILL, Howard. "Rochester: Augustan or Explorer?" *Pinto Festschrift*, pp. 51-64.

6   FUJIMURA, Thomas H. "Rochester's 'Satyr against Mankind': An Analysis." *SP*, 55(1958):576-90.

7   GIDDEY, Ernest. "Rochester, poète baroque (1647-1680)." *Études de Lettres*, 7(1964):155-64.

8   HAM, Roswell G. "The Authorship of *A Session of the Poets* (1677)." *RES*, 9(1933):319-22. [Argues for Settle's authorship.]

9   HOOK, Lucyle. "The Publication Date of Rochester's *Valentinian.*" *HLQ*, 19(1956):401-07.

10 HOOK, Lucyle. "Something More about Rochester." *MLN*, 75(1960):478-85. [References in letters of Godfrey Thacker.]

11 LEGOUIS, Pierre. "Rochester et sa réputation." *EA*, 1(1937):53-69.

12 MAIN, C. F. "The Right Vein of Rochester's *Satyr.*" *Essays in Literary History Presented to J. Milton French*. New Brunswick, N.J., 1960, pp. 93-112.

13 MOORE, John F. "The Originality of Rochester's *Satyr against Mankind.*" *PMLA*, 58(1943):393-401.

14 PINTO, Vivian de Sola. *Rochester: Portrait of a Restoration Poet.* 1935. Rev. ed.: *Enthusiast in Wit: A Portrait of John Wilmot, Earl of Rochester 1647-1680*. Lincoln, Neb., 1962.*

15 PRINZ, Johannes. *John Wilmot, Earl of Rochester, His Life and Writings, with his Lordship's Private Correspondence, Various Other Documents, and a Bibliography of His Works and of the Literature on Him.* Leipzig, 1927.

16 RIGHTER, Anne. "John Wilmot, Earl of Rochester." *PBA*, 53(1967):47-69.

17 TODD, William B. "The 1680 Editions of Rochester's *Poems* with Notes on Earlier Texts." *PBSA*, 47(1953):43-58.

18 VIETH, David M. *Attribution in Restoration Poetry: A Study of Rochester's "Poems" of 1680*. New Haven, 1963.

19 WHITFIELD, Francis. *Beast in View. A Study of the Earl of Rochester's Poetry.* Cambridge, Mass., 1936.

1 WILLIAMS, Charles. *Rochester.* 1935.

2 WILSON, J. Harold. "Rochester's 'A Session of the Poets.' " *RES*, 22(1946): 109–16. [Arguments for Rochester's authorship.]

3 WILSON, J. Harold. "Rochester's *Valentinian* and Heroic Sentiment." *ELH*, 4(1937):265–73.

4 WILSON, J. Harold. "Satiric Elements in Rochester's *Valentinian.*" *PQ*, 16(1937):41–48.

Roscommon, Wentworth Dillon, Earl of (1633?–1685)

5 NIEMEYER, Carl. "The Birth Date of the Earl of Roscommon." *RES*, 9(1933):449–51.

6 NIEMEYER, Carl. "The Earl of Roscommon's Academy." *MLN*, 49(1934): 432–37.

7 NIEMEYER, Carl. "A Roscommon Canon." *SP*, 36(1939):622–36.

8 STUART, D. M. "Roscommon of the 'Unspotted Bays.' " *English*, 1(1936): 140–50.

Sedley, Sir Charles (1639–1701)

9 *Poetical and Dramatic Works*, ed. V. de Sola Pinto. 2 vols. 1928.

10 BODDY, Margaret P. "The 1692 *Fourth Book of Virgil.*" *RES*, n.s. 15(1964): 364–80.

11 PINTO, V. de Sola. *Sir Charles Sedley, 1639–1701: A Study in the Life and Literature of the Restoration.* 1927.

Stanley, Thomas (1625–1678)

12 *Poems and Translations*, ed. Galbraith Miller Crump. Oxford, 1962.

BIBLIOGRAPHY

13 FLOWER, Margaret. "Thomas Stanley (1625–1678): A Bibliography of His Writings in Prose and Verse (1647–1743)." *TCBS*, 1(1950):139–72.

1   CRUMP, Galbraith M. "Thomas Stanley's Manuscript of his Poems and Translations." *TCBS*, 2(1958):359–65.

2   O'REGAN, M. J. "The French Source of Thomas Stanley's Paraphrases of Psalms 139 and 148." *MLR*, 59(1964):179–81.

3   WILSON, Edward M., and E. R. VINCENT. "Thomas Stanley's Translations and Borrowings from Spanish and Italian Poems." *RLC*, 32(1958):548–56.

Tate, Nahum (1652–1715)

4   BLACK, James. "The Influence of Hobbes on Nahum Tate's *King Lear*" *SEL*, 7(1967):377–85.

5   BLACK, James. "An Augustan Stage-History: Nahum Tate's *King Lear*." *RECTR*, 6, No. 1 (1967):36–54.

6   GOLDEN, Samuel. "The Late Seventeenth-Century Writer and the Laureateship: Nahum Tate's Tenure." *Hermathena*, 89(1957):30–38.

7   GOLDEN, Samuel. "The Three Faithful Teates." *N&Q*, 200(1955):374–80.

8   SCOTT-THOMAS, H. F. "Nahum Tate and the Seventeenth Century." *ELH*, 1(1934):250–75.

9   SPENCER, Christopher. "A Word for Tate's *King Lear*." *SEL*, 3(1963):241–51.

10 WILLIAMS, T. D. Duncan. "Mr. Nahum Tate's *King Lear*." *SN*, 38(1966):290–300.

Walsh, William (1663–1708)

11 FREEMAN, Phyllis. "Two Fragments of Walsh Manuscripts." *RES*, n.s. 8(1957):390–401.

12 FREEMAN, Phyllis. "Who Was Sir Roger de Coverley?" *Quarterly Review*, 285(1947):592–604. [Proposes Walsh as the "original" for Sir Roger.]

13 FREEMAN, Phyllis. "William Walsh and Dryden: Recently Discovered Letters." *RES*, 24(1948):195–202.

14 FREEMAN, Phyllis. "William Walsh's Letters and Poems in *MS. Malone 9*." *Bodleian Quarterly Record*, 7(1934):503–07.

1 SAMBROOK, A. J. "William Walsh and *The Golden Age from the Fourth Eclogue of Virgil* (1703)." *MP*, 64(1967):324–25.

2 VETTER, Dale B. "William Walsh's 'In Defence of Painting.'" *MLN*, 66(1951):518–23.

Drama

(London is to be assumed as place of publication, unless otherwise noted).

Bibliography

3 LANGHANS, Edward A. "Restoration Theatre Scholarship 1960–66: A Résumé and Suggestions for Future Work." *RECTR*, 6(1967):8–11.

4 SUMMERS, Montague. *A Bibliography of the Restoration Drama*. 1935.

5 WILSON, Stuart. "Restoration and Eighteenth Century Theatre Research Bibliography for 1935–1939." *RECTR*, 5(1966):40–58.

6 WOODWARD, Gertrude L., and James G. McMANAWAY. *A Check List of English Plays, 1641–1700*. Chicago, 1945. [*Supplement* by Fredson Bowers, Charlottesville, 1949.]

General Studies

7 AVERY, Emmett L. "The Restoration Audience." *PQ*, 45(1966):54–61.

8 AVERY, Emmett L. "Rhetorical Patterns in Restoration Prologues and Epilogues." *Essays in American and English Literature Presented to Bruce Robert McElderry, Jr.*, ed. Max F. Schulz and others. Athens, Ohio, 1967, pp. 221–37.

9 BORGMAN, Albert S. *The Life and Death of William Mountfort*. Cambridge, Mass., 1935.

10 BOSWELL, Eleanore. *The Restoration Court Stage, 1660–1702*. Cambridge, Mass., 1932. Repr. 1967.

11 BRUSTEIN, Robert. "The Monstrous Regiment of Women: Sources for the Satiric View of the Court Lady in English Drama." *Pinto Festschrift*, pp. 38–50.

12 CLARK, William S. *The Early Irish Stage: The Beginnings to 1720*. Oxford, 1955.

13 CLINTON-BADDELEY, V. C. *The Burlesque Tradition in the English Theatre after 1660*. 1952.

14 CUNNINGHAM, John E. *Restoration Drama*. 1966.

1 DOWNES, John. *Roscius Anglicanus* (1708) ed. Montague Summers. 1929. ed. John LOFTIS (ARS). Los Angeles, 1969.

2 HARBAGE, Alfred. *Annals of English Drama, 975–1700*. . . . Philadelphia, 1940. [Rev. ed. by S. Schoenbaum, 1964].

3 HARBAGE, Alfred. *Cavalier Drama: An Historical and Critical Supplement to the Study of the Elizabethan and Restoration Stage*. New York, 1936.

4 HOTSON, Leslie. *The Commonwealth and Restoration Stage*. Cambridge, Mass., 1928.

5 HOY, Cyrus. "The Effect of the Restoration on Drama." *TSL*, 6(1961):85–91.

6 LOFTIS, John, ed. *Restoration Drama: Modern Essays in Criticism*. New York, 1966.†

7 *The London Stage, 1660–1800: A Calendar of Plays, Entertainments & Afterpieces together with Casts, Box-Receipts and Contemporary Comment, Compiled from the Playbills, Newspapers and Theatrical Diaries of the Period.* Part I: *1660–1700*, ed. William Van Lennep, with a Critical Introduction by Emmett L. Avery and Arthur H. Scouten. Carbondale, Ill., 1965.*

8 MINER, Earl, ed. *Restoration Dramatists: A Collection of Critical Essays.* Englewood Cliffs, N.J., 1966.†

9 MOORE, Robert E. *Henry Purcell and the Restoration Theatre*. Cambridge, Mass., 1961.

10 NICOLL, Allardyce. *A History of Restoration Drama 1660–1700*. Cambridge, 1923. [Rev. ed.: *A History of English Drama, 1660–1900*. 6 vols. 1952–59. Vol. I: *1660–1700*.]*

11 NOYES, Robert G. *Ben Jonson on the English Stage, 1660–1776*. Cambridge, Mass., 1935.

12 NOYES, Robert G. "Contemporary Musical Settings of the Songs in Restoration Drama." *ELH*, 1(1934):323–44.

13 NOYES, Robert G. "Songs from Restoration Drama in Contemporary and Eighteenth-Century Poetical Miscellanies." *ELH*, 3(1936):291–316.

14 NOYES, Robert G., and Roy LAMSON, Jr. "Broadside-Ballad Versions of the Songs in Restoration Drama." *HSNPL*, 19(1937):199–218.

15 ROSENFELD, Sybil. *Strolling Players and Drama in the Provinces, 1660–1765*. Cambridge, 1939.

16 SINGH, Sarup. *The Theory of Drama in the Restoration Period*. Calcutta, 1963.

17 SMITH, Dane F. *The Critics in the Audience of the London Theatres from Buckingham to Sheridan: A Study of Neoclassicism in the Playhouse, 1671–1779*. Albuquerque, 1953.

18 SMITH, Dane F. *Plays about the Theatre in England from "The Rehearsal" in 1671 to the Licensing Act in 1737*. . . . New York, 1936.

19 SORELIUS, Gunnar. *"The Giant Race before the Flood": Pre-Restoration Drama on the Stage and in the Criticism of the Restoration*. Uppsala, 1966.

1 SOUTHERN, Richard. *Changeable Scenery: Its Origin and Development in the British Theatre.* 1952.

2 SPEAIGHT, George. *The History of the English Puppet Theatre.* London and New York, 1955.

3 SUMMERS, Montague. *The Playhouse of Pepys.* 1935.

4 SUMMERS, Montague. *The Restoration Theatre.* 1934.

5 WHITING, George W. "Political Satire in London Stage Plays, 1680–83." *MP*, 28(1930):29–43.

6 WILSON, J. Harold. *All the King's Ladies: Actresses of the Restoration.* Chicago, 1958.

7 WILSON, J. Harold. *Mr. Goodman, the Player.* Pittsburgh, 1964. [Cardell Goodman.]

8 WILSON, J. Harold. *A Preface to Restoration Drama.* Boston, 1965.† Repr. Cambridge, Mass., 1968.

9 WILSON, J. Harold. "Rant, Cant, and Tone on the Restoration Stage." *SP*, 52(1955):592–98.

Comedy

BIBLIOGRAPHY

10 JONES, Claude E. "Molière in England to 1775: A Checklist." *N&Q*, 202 (1957):383–89.

11 PAINE, Clarence S. *The Comedy of Manners (1660–1700): A Reference Guide to the Comedy of the Restoration.* Boston, 1941.

GENERAL STUDIES

12 ALLEMAN, Gellert S. *Matrimonial Law and the Materials of Restoration Comedy.* Philadelphia, 1942.

13 B[ATESON], F. W. "Contributions to a Dictionary of Critical Terms: 1. Comedy of Manners." *EIC*, 1(1951):89–93.

14 BERKELEY, David S. "The Art of 'Whining' Love." *SP*, 52(1955):478–96.

15 BERKELEY, David S. "The Penitent Rake in Restoration Comedy." *MP*, 49(1952):223–33.

16 BERKELEY, David S. *The Précieuse, or Distressed Heroine of Restoration Comedy.* Stillwater, Okla., 1959.

17 BERKELEY, David S. "Some Notes on Probability in Restoration Drama." *N&Q*, 200(1955):237–39, 342–44, 432.

18 CECIL, C. D. "Delicate and Indelicate Puns in Restoration Comedy." *MLR*, 61(1966):572–78.

19 CECIL, C. D. "Une Espèce d'éloquence abrégé: The Idealized Speech of that Country." *EA*, 19(1966):15–25.

20 CECIL, C. D. "Libertine and Précieuse Elements in Restoration Comedy." *EIC*, 9(1959):239–53.

1 CECIL, C. D. "Raillery in Restoration Comedy." *HLQ*, 29(1966):147–59.

2 DOBRÉE, Bonamy. *Restoration Comedy, 1660–1720.* Oxford, 1924.

3 FUJIMURA, Thomas H. *The Restoration Comedy of Wit.* Princeton, 1952.*

4 GAGEN, Jean E. *The New Woman: Her Emergence in English Drama, 1600–1730.* New York, 1954.

5 HAZLITT, William. *Lectures on the English Comic Writers.* Lecture IV: *On Wycherley, Congreve, Vanbrugh, and Farquhar.* 1819. (EL.) 1910.

6 HOLLAND, Norman H. *The First Modern Comedies: The Significance of Etherege, Wycherley, and Congreve.* Cambridge, Mass., 1959.*

7 KNIGHTS, L. C. "Restoration Comedy: The Reality and the Myth." *Explorations: Essays in Criticism Mainly on Literature of the Seventeenth Century* (1946), pp. 131–49. [See also F. W. Bateson, "L. C. Knights and Restoration Comedy." *EIC*, 7(1957):56–67.]

8 LAMB, Charles. "On the Artificial Comedy of the Last Century." *Essays of Elia.* [Originally appeared in *London Magazine*, April 1822, and frequently repr., e.g., in *Charles Lamb and Elia*, ed. J. E. Morpurgo. 1948, pp. 224–32.]†

9 LEECH, Clifford. "Restoration Comedy: The Earlier Phase." *EIC*, 1(1951):165–84.

10 LEGOUIS, P., *et al.* "Les voies de la critique récente: Comment elle étudie la comédie de la Restauration." *EA*, 19(1966):412–23.

11 LYNCH, Kathleen M. *The Social Mode of Restoration Comedy.* New York, 1926.

12 MACAULAY, Thomas Babington. "Comic Dramatists of the Restoration." *Edinburgh Review*, 72 (1841), 490–528. [Frequently repr. Ostensibly a review of *The Dramatic Works of Wycherley, Congreve, Vanbrugh and Farquhar, with Biographical and Critical Notices*, by Leigh Hunt, 1840.]

13 McDONALD, Charles O. "Restoration Comedy as Drama of Satire: An Investigation into Seventeenth-Century Aesthetics." *SP*, 61(1964):522–44.

14 MANDACH, André de. *Molière et la comédie de moeurs en Angleterre (1660–68): Essai de littérature comparée.* Neuchâtel, 1946.

15 MIGNON, Elizabeth. *Crabbed Age and Youth: The Old Men and Women in the Restoration Comedy of Manners.* Durham, N.C., 1946.

16 MONTGOMERY, Guy. "The Challenge of Restoration Comedy." *University of California Publications in English*, Vol. I. Berkeley, 1929, pp. 133–51.

17 PALMER, John. *The Comedy of Manners.* 1913.

18 PERKINSON, Richard H. "Topographical Comedy in the Seventeenth Century." *ELH*, 3(1936):270–90.

19 PERRY, Henry Ten Eyck. *The Comic Spirit in Restoration Drama*, New Haven, 1925.

20 SCOUTEN, A. H. "Notes toward a History of Restoration Comedy." *PQ.* 45(1966):62–70.

1 SHARMA, R. C. *Themes and Conventions in the Comedy of Manners.* New York, 1965.

2 SIMON, Irène. "Restoration Comedy and the Critics." *RLV*, 29(1963):397–430. [Review article.]

3 SMITH, John Harrington. "French Sources for Six English Comedies, 1660–1750." *JEGP*, 47(1948):390–94. [*The Woman-Captain* by Shadwell; *The She-Gallants* by Granville; *The Beau Defeated* by Mary Pix; *Injured Love; The Coquet* by Charles Molloy; and *A Tutor for the Beaus* by Hewitt.]

4 SMITH, John Harrington. *The Gay Couple in Restoration Comedy.* Cambridge, Mass., 1948.

5 STOLL, Elmer E. "The 'Real Society' in Restoration Comedy: Hymeneal Pretenses." *MLN*, 58(1943):175–81.

6 SUCKLING, Norman. "Molière and English Restoration Comedy." *Restoration Theatre*, ed. John Russell Brown and Bernard Harris. (Stratford-upon-Avon Studies, 6.) London and New York, 1965, pp. 93–107.

7 TRAUGOTT, John. "The Rake's Progress from Court to Comedy: A Study in Comic Form." *SEL*, 6(1966):381–407.

8 VERNON, P. F. "Marriage of Convenience and the Mode of Restoration Comedy." *EIC*, 12(1962):370–87.

9 WILCOX, John. *The Relation of Molière to Restoration Comedy.* New York, 1938.

10 WILKINSON, D. R. M. *The Comedy of Habit: An Essay on the Use of Courtesy Literature in a Study of Restoration Comic Drama.* The Hague, 1964.

Heroic Play and Tragedy

11 DOBRÉE, Bonamy, ed. *Five Heroic Plays.* (WC.) 1960. (Orrery, *Mustapha*; Settle, *Empress of Morocco*; Crowne, *Destruction of Jerusalem*, Part II; Lee, *Sophonisba*; Dryden, *Aureng-Zebe*.)

12 CHASE, Lewis N. *The English Heroic Play: A Critical Description of the Rhymed Tragedy of the Restoration.* New York, 1903. Repr. New York, 1965.

13 CLARK, William S. "The Sources of the Restoration Heroic Play." *RES*, 4(1928):49–63.

14 CLARK, William S. "The Definition of the 'Heroic Play' in the Restoration Period." *RES*, 8(1932):437–44.

15 DEANE, Cecil V. *Dramatic Theory and the Rhymed Heroic Play.* 1931.

16 DOBRÉE, Bonamy. *Restoration Tragedy, 1660–1720.* Oxford, 1929.

17 LEECH, Clifford. "Restoration Tragedy: A Reconsideration." *DUJ*, 42(1950):106–15.

18 LYNCH, Kathleen. "Conventions of Platonic Drama in the Heroic Plays of Orrery and Dryden." *PMLA*, 44(1929):456–71. [Cf. William S. Clark, "The Platonic Element in the Restoration Heroic Play." *PMLA*, 45(1930):623–24, and reply by K. Lynch, pp. 625–26.]

19 NOYES, Robert G. "Conventions of Song in Restoration Tragedy." *PMLA*, 53(1938):162–88.

20 PARSONS, A. E. "The English Heroic Play." *MLR*, 33(1938):1–14.

21 RIGHTER, Anne. "Heroic Tragedy." *Restoration Theatre.* ed. John Russell Brown and Bernard Harris (Stratford-upon-Avon Studies, 6.) London and New York, 1965, pp. 135–57.

22 ROTHSTEIN, Eric. *Restoration Tragedy: Form and the Process of Change.* Madison, Wis., 1967.

23 WILSON, John Harold. *A Preface to Restoration Tragedy.* Cambridge, Mass., 1968.

Adaptations of Shakespeare

1   MACEY, Samuel L. "Duffett's *Mock Tempest* and the Assimilation of Shakespeare during the Restoration & Eighteenth Century." *RECTR*, 7, No. 1(1968):44–52.

2   MERCHANT, M. Moelwyn. "Shakespeare 'Made Fit.' " *Restoration Theatre*, ed. John Russell Brown and Bernard Harris (Stratford-upon-Avon Studies, 6.) London and New York, 1965, pp. 195–219.

3   ODELL, George C. D. *Shakespeare from Betterton to Irving.* 2 vols. New York, 1920.†

4   SPENCER, Christopher, ed. *Five Restoration Adaptations of Shakespeare.* Urbana, 1965. [*Macbeth* (Sir William Davenant), the operatic version of *The Tempest*, *King Lear* (Tate), *Richard III* (Cibber), *The Jew of Venice* (Granville).]

5   SPENCER, Hazelton. *Shakespeare Improved: The Restoration Versions in Quarto and on the Stage.* Cambridge, Mass., 1927.

6   SPRAGUE, Arthur Colby. *Shakespeare and the Actors: The Stage Business in His Plays, 1660–1905.* Cambridge, Mass., 1944.

7   SPRAGUE, Arthur Colby. *Shakespearian Players and Performances.* Cambridge, Mass., 1953; London, 1954.

Opera

8   DENT, Edward J. *Foundations of English Opera: A Study of Musical Drama in England During the Seventeenth Century.* Cambridge, 1928.

9   LINCOLN, Stoddard. "Eccles and Congreve: Music and Drama on the Restoration Stage." *Theatre Notebook*, 18(1963):7–18.

10   LOEWENBERG, Alfred. *Annals of Opera, 1597–1940. Compiled from the Original Sources.* Cambridge, 1943. 2nd ed. rev. and corr. 2 vols. Geneva, 1955.

11   NOYES, Robert Gale. "Contemporary Musical Settings of the Songs in Restoration Dramatic Operas." *HSNPL*, 20(1938):99–121.

12   WALMSLEY, D. M. "The Influence of Foreign Opera on English Operatic Plays of the Restoration Period." *Anglia*, 52(1928):37–50.

13   WHITE, Eric W. *The Rise of English Opera.* 1951.

The Collier Controversy

14   ANTHONY, Sister Rose. *The Jeremy Collier Stage Controversy, 1698–1726.* Milwaukee, 1937.

15   KRUTCH, Joseph Wood. *Comedy and Conscience after the Restoration.* New York., 1924.†

Banks, John (*c. 1650–c. 1720*)

1 *The Unhappy Favourite, or the Earl of Essex*, ed. Thomas M. H. Blair. New York, 1939.

2 BOWERS, Fredson. "The Variant Sheets in John Banks's *Cyrus the Great*, 1696." *SB*, 4(1951–52):174–82.

3 HOCHULI, Hans. *John Banks, eine Studie zum Drama des späten 17. Jahrhunderts. Der Übergang vom höfischen Spätbarock zum bürgerlichen Klassizismus.* Bern, 1952.

4 KNEPLER, Henry W. "Maxwell Anderson: A Historical Parallel— Problems for the Poetic Dramatist." *Queen's Quarterly*, 64(1957):250–63. [Parallels between plays of Banks and Anderson.]

Behn, Aphra (*1640–1689*)

5 *The Rover*, ed. Frederick Link. [RRestDS] Lincoln, Neb., 1966.†

6 DAY, Robert A. "Aphra Behn's First Biography." *SB*, 22(1969):227–40.

7 LINK, Frederick M. *Aphra Behn*. New York, 1968.

Buckingham, George Villiers, Duke of (*1628–1687*)

8 *The Critic* [by Sheridan] and *The Rehearsal*, ed. Cedric Gale. Woodbury, New York, 1960.†

9 CHAPMAN, Hester W. *Great Villiers: A Study of George Villiers, Second Duke of Buckingham, 1628–1687.* 1949.

10 CLINTON-BADDELEY, V. C. *The Burlesque Tradition in the English Theatre after 1660.* 1952.

11 WILSON, John Harold. *A Rake and His Times: George Villiers, 2nd Duke of Buckingham.* New York and London, 1954.

Congreve, William (*1670–1729*)

12 *Comedies*, ed. Bonamy Dobrée. (WC.) 1925.

1 *Complete Plays*, ed. Herbert Davis. (Curtain Playwright Editions.) Chicago, 1957.

2 *Complete Plays*, ed. Alexander C. Ewald. (Mermaid Series.) 1887, 1903.†

3 *Complete Works*, ed. Montague Summers. 4 vols. 1923.

4 *Incognita and the Way of the World*, ed. A. Norman Jeffares. 1966.

5 *Love for Love*, ed. Emmett L. Avery. (RRestDS.) Lincoln, Neb., 1966.†

6 *The Mourning Bride, Poems, and Miscellanies*, ed. Bonamy Dobrée. (WC.) 1928.

7 *The Way of the World*, ed. Kathleen M. Lynch. (RRestDS.) Lincoln, Neb., 1965.†

8 *William Congreve: Letters and Documents*, ed. John C. Hodges. New York, 1964.

9 *Works*, ed. F. W. Bateson. 1930. [Comedies, *Incognita*, and Selected Poems.]

BIBLIOGRAPHY

10 DOBRÉE, Bonamy. *William Congreve*. (WTW.) 1963.

11 AVERY, Emmett L. *Congreve's Plays on the Eighteenth-Century Stage*. New York, 1951.

12 BARNARD, John. "Did Congreve Write *A Satyr against Love?*" *Bull. N.Y. Pub. Lib.*, 68(1964): 308–22. [With text of the *Satyr*.]

13 GAGEN, Jean. "Congreve's Mirabell and the Ideal of the Gentleman." *PMLA*, 79(1964):422–27.

14 GOSSE, Anthony. "The Omitted Scene in Congreve's *Love for Love*." *MP*, 61(1963):40–42.

15 GOSSE, Anthony. "Plot and Character in Congreve's *Double Dealer*." *MLQ*, 29(1968):274–88.

16 GOSSE, Edmund. *Life of William Congreve*. 1888. Rev. ed., 1924.

17 HODGES, John C. "The Ballad in Congreve's *Love for Love*." *PMLA*, 48(1933):953–54.

18 HODGES, John C. "The Composition of Congreve's *Mourning Bride*." *PMLA*, 58(1943):971–76.

19 HODGES, John C. *The Library of William Congreve*. New York, 1955.

20 HODGES, John C. *William Congreve the Man: A Biography from New Sources*. New York, 1941.*

21 HOWARTH, R. G. "Congreve and Anne Bracegirdle." *ESA*, 4(1961):159–61.

22 LEECH, Clifford. "Congreve and the Century's End." *PQ*, 41(1962): 275–93.

1 LYNCH, Kathleen M. *A Congreve Gallery*. Cambridge, Mass., 1951.

2 LYONS, Charles R. "Congreve's Miracle of Love." *Criticism*, 6(1964):331–48. [*Love for Love.*]

3 MAUROCORDATO, Alexandre. "Ainsi va le monde: étude sur la structure d'une 'comedy of manners.'" *Archives des Lettres Modernes*, No. 76. (1967): pp. 1–54. [*The Way of the World.*]

4 MUESCHKE, Paul and Miriam. *A New View of Congreve's "Way of the World."* Ann Arbor, 1958.

5 MUIR, Kenneth. "The Comedies of William Congreve." *Restoration Theatre*. ed. John Russell Brown and Bernard Harris. (Stratford-upon-Avon Studies, 6.) London and New York, 1965, pp. 221–37.

6 NOLAN, Paul T. "Congreve's Lovers: Art and the Critic." *DramS*, 1(1962):330–39.

7 NOLAN, Paul T. "*The Way of the World:* Congreve's Moment of Truth." *Southern Speech Journal*, 25(1959):75–95.

8 NOYES, Robert G. "Congreve and His Comedies in the Eighteenth-Century Novel." *PQ*, 39(1960):464–80.

9 POTTER, Elmer B. "The Paradox of Congreve's *Mourning Bride*." *PMLA*, 58(1943):977–1001.

10 PROTOPOPESCO, Dragos. *Un Classique moderne: William Congreve, sa vie, son oeuvre*. 1924.

16 SMITH, John Harrington. "Thomas Corneille to Betterton to Congreve." *JEGP*, 45(1946):209–13. [*The Way of the World.*]

12 TAYLOR, D. Crane. *William Congreve*. 1931.

13 TURNER, Darwin T. "The Servant in the Comedies of William Congreve." *CLAJ*, 1(1958):68–74.

14 VAN VORIS, William H. *The Cultivated Stance: The Designs of Congreve's Plays*. Dublin and London, 1965.

15 WILLIAMS, Aubrey. "Poetical Justice: The Contrivances of Providence and the Works of William Congreve." *ELH*, 35(1968):540–65.

Crowne, John (d. 1703)

16 *City Politiques*, ed. John H. Wilson. [RRestDS.] Lincoln, Neb., 1967.†

17 *Sir Courtly Nice*, ed. Charlotte B. Hughes. The Hague, 1966.

18 BOSWELL, Eleanore. *The Restoration Court Stage (1660–1702), with a Particular Account of the Production of "Calisto."* Cambridge, Mass., 1932.

19 WHITE, Arthur F. *John Crowne: His Life and Dramatic Works*. Cleveland, 1922.

20 WINSHIP, George P. *The First Harvard Playwright: A Bibliography of the Restoration Dramatist John Crowne, with Extracts from His Prefaces and the Earlier Version of the Epilogue to "Sir Courtley Nice."* Cambridge, Mass., 1922.

Davenant, Sir William (1660–1668)

1 BERRY, Herbert. "Three New Poems by Davenant." *PQ*, 31(1952):70–74.

2 COLLINS, Howard S. *The Comedy of Sir William Davenant*. The Hague, 1967.

3 DOWLIN, C. M. *Sir William Davenant's 'Gondibert': Its Preface and Hobbes's Answer*. Philadelphia, 1934.

4 DUST, Alvin I. "The *Seventh and Last Canto of Gondibert* and Two Dedicatory Poems." *JEGP*, 60(1961):282–85.

5 FEIL, J. P. "Davenant Exonerated." *MLR*, 58(1963):335–42.

6 GIBBS, A. M. "A Davenant Imitation of Donne?" *RES*, n.s. 18(1967): 45–49.

7 HARBAGE, Alfred. *Sir William Davenant, Poet Venturer, 1606–1668*. Philadelphia, 1935.

8 KAUFMANN, R. J. "Suckling and Davenant Satirized by Brome." *MLR*, 55(1960):332–44.

9 NETHERCOT, Arthur H. *Sir William D'Avenant, Poet Laureate and Playwright-Manager*. Chicago, 1938; New York, 1967 [with additional notes].*

10 SPENCER, Christopher. *Davenant's "Macbeth" from the Yale Manuscript: An Edition, with a Discussion of the Relation of Davenant's Text to Shakespeare's*. New Haven, 1961.

11 SPENCER, Hazelton. "D'Avenant's *Macbeth* and Shakespeare's." *PMLA*, 40(1925):619–44.

12 SQUIER, Charles L. "Davenant's Comic Assault on *Préciosité*: The Platonic Lovers." *University of Colorado Studies in Language and Literature*, 10 (1966):57–72.

D'Urfey, Thomas (1653–1723)

13 *The Songs of Thomas D'Urfey*, ed. Cyrus L. Day. Cambridge, Mass., 1933.

14 *Wit and Mirth; Or, Pills to Purge Melancholy* [1719–20], with Introduction by Cyrus L. Day. 6 vols. in 3. New York, 1959. [Facsimile of 1876 reprint.]

15 *Wonders in the Sun, or The Kingdom of the Birds* [1706], ed. William W. Appleton. (ARS, 104.) Los Angeles, 1964.

16 BISWANGER, Raymond A., Jr. "Thomas D'Urfey's *Richmond Heiress* (1693): A Bibliographical Study." *SB*, 5(1952–53):169–78.

1 BOWERS, Fredson. "Thomas D'Urfey's 'Comical History of Don Quixote.' 1694." *PBSA*, 43(1949):191–95.

2 DAY, Cyrus L. *Dates and Performances of Thomas D'Urfey's Plays.* Charlottesville, 1950.

3 DAY, Cyrus L. "*Pills to Purge Melancholy.*" *RES*, 8(1932):177–84.

4 ELLIS, William D., Jr. "Thomas D'Urfey, the Pope-Philips Quarrel, and *The Shepherd's Week.*" *PMLA*, 74(1959):203–12.

5 FORSYTHE, Robert S. *A Study of the Plays of Thomas D'Urfey, with a Reprint of "A Fool's Preferment."* (Western Reserve University Bulletins, Vol. 19, No. 5; Vol. 20, No. 5), 1916–17.

6 GRAHAM, C. B. "The Jonsonian Tradition in the Comedies of Thomas D'Urfey." *MLQ*, 8(1947):47–52.

7 LEGMAN, G. "*Pills to Purge Melancholy*: A Bibliographical Note." *Midwest Folklore*, 9(1959):89–102.

8 LYNCH, Kathleen M. "Thomas D'Urfey's Contribution to Sentimental Comedy." *PQ*, 9(1930):249–59.

9 VAUGHN, Jack A. "A D'Urfey Play Dated." *MP*, 64(1967):322–23. [*A Fond Husband.*]

10 VAUGHN, Jack A. " 'Persevering, Unexhausted Bard': Tom D'Urfey." *QJS*, 53(1967):342–48.

Etherege, Sir George (1635?–1691)

11 *Letterbook*, ed. Sybil Rosenfeld. 1928.

12 *The Man of Mode*, ed. W. B. Carnochan. (RRestDS.) Lincoln, Neb., 1966.†

13 *Poems*, ed. James Thorpe. Princeton, 1963.

14 *Works*, ed. H. F. B. Brett-Smith. Vols. I–II: *Plays.* Oxford, 1927.

15 AUFFRET, J. M. "The Man of Mode and The Plain Dealer: Common Origin and Parallels." *EA*, 19(1966):209–22.

16 BOSWELL, Eleanore. "Sir George Etherege." *RES*, 7(1931):207–09.

17 BOYETTE, Purvis E. "The Songs of George Etherege." *SEL*, 6(1966):409–19.

18 BRACHER, Frederick. "The Letterbooks of Sir George Etherege." *HLB*, 15 (1967):238–45.

19 BRACHER, Frederick. "Sir George Etherege and His Secretary." *HLB*, 15 (1967):331–44.

20 COX, R. S., Jr. "Richard Flecknoe and *The Man of Mode.*" *MLQ*, 29(1968):182–89.

1 DOBRÉE, Bonamy. *Essays in Biography, 1680–1726."* 1925. [Pp. 1–56: "His Excellency Sir George Etherege."]

2 FUJIMURA, Thomas H. "Etherege at Constantinople." *PMLA,* 62(1956): 465–81.

3 HAYMAN, John G. "Dorimant and the Comedy of a Man of Mode." *MLQ,* 30(1969):183–97.

4 KRAUSE, David. "The Defaced Angel: Satanic Grace in *The Man of Mode."* *DramS,* 7(1969):87–103.

5 MacCAMIC, Frances S. *Sir George Etherege: A Study in Restoration Comedy, 1660–1680.* Cedar Rapids, Iowa, 1931.

6 POWELL, Jocelyn. "George Etherege and the Form of a Comedy." *Restoration Theatre,* ed. John Russell Brown and Bernard Harris (Stratford-upon-Avon Studies, 6.) London and New York, 1965, pp. 43–69.

7 ROSENFELD, Sybil. "Sir George Etherege in Ratisbon." *RES,* 10(1934): 177–89.

8 ROSENFELD, Sybil. "The Second Letterbook of Sir George Etherege.' *RES,* n.s. 3(1952):19–27.

9 UNDERWOOD, Dale. *Etherege and the Seventeenth-Century Comedy of Manners.* New Haven, 1957.*

Farquhar, George (1678–1707)

10 *The Beaux' Stratagem,* ed. Vincent F. Hopper and Gerald B. Lahey. Great Neck, New York, 1963.†

11 *The Beaux' Stratagem,* ed. Eric Rothstein. New York, 1966.†

12 *Complete Works,* ed. Charles Stonehill. 2 vols. 1930. Repr. New York, 1967.

13 *Farquhar,* ed. William Archer. (Mermaid Series.) 1906. Repr. New York, 1959.†

14 *The Recruiting Officer,* ed. Michael Shugrue. (RRestDS.) Lincoln, Neb., 1965.†

BIBLIOGRAPHY

15 FARMER, A. J. *George Farquhar.* (WTW.) 1966.

16 CONNELY, Willard. *Young George Farquhar: The Restoration Drama at Twilight.* 1949.

17 JAMES, Eugene N. "The Burlesque of Restoration Comedy in *Love and a Bottle." SEL,* 5(1965):469–90.

18 ROTHSTEIN, Eric. *George Farquhar.* New York, 1967.

1 SPINNER, Kaspar. *George Farquhar als Dramatiker*. Bern, 1956.

2 SUTHERLAND, James R. "New Light on George Farquhar." *TLS*, March 6, 1937, p. 171. [See also Peter Kavanagh, *TLS*, Feb. 10, 1945, p. 72.]

Howard, Sir Robert (1626–1698)

3 *The Committee*, ed. C. N. Thurber. Urbana, 1921.

4 *Dryden and Howard, 1664–1668: The Text of an Essay of Dramatic Poesy, The Indian Emperor and The Duke of Lerma, with Other Controversial Matter*, ed. D[ennis] D. Arundell. Cambridge, 1929.

5 OLIVER, H. J. *Sir Robert Howard (1626–1698): A Critical Biography*. Durham, N.C., 1963.

6 ROSCIONI, Gian Carlo. "Sir Robert Howard's 'Sceptical Curiosity.'" *MP*, 65(1967):53–59.

Lee, Nathaniel (1649?–1692)

7 *Works*, ed. Thomas B. Stroup and Arthur L. Cooke. 2 vols. New Brunswick, N. J., and London, 1954–55.

8 *Lucius Junius Brutus*, ed. John Loftis. (RRestDS.) Lincoln, Neb., 1967.†

9 BOWERS, Fredson. "Nathaniel Lee: Three Probable Seventeenth-Century Piracies." *PBSA*, 44(1950):62–66.

10 HAM, Roswell G. *Otway and Lee: Biography for a Baroque Age*. New Haven, 1931.

Motteux, Peter Anthony (1663–1718)

BIBLIOGRAPHY

11 CUNNINGHAM, Robert N. "A Bibliography of the Writings of Peter Anthony Motteux." *Proceedings Oxford Bibliographical Society*, 3 (1933): 317–37, 368.

12 BOWERS, Fredson. "Motteux's 'Love's a Jest' (1696): A Running-Title and Presswork Problem." *PBSA*, 48(1954):268–73.

1 CUNNINGHAM, Robert N. *Peter Anthony Motteux, 1663–1718: A Biographical and Critical Study.* Oxford, 1933.

2 WIEDER, Robert. *Pierre Motteux et les débuts du journalisme en Angleterre au XVIIᵉ siècle.* 1944.

Orrery, Roger Boyle, Earl of (*1621–1679*)

3 *Dramatic Works,* ed. William S. Clark II. 2 vols. Cambridge, Mass., 1937

4 LYNCH, Kathleen M. *Roger Boyle, First Earl of Orrery.* Knoxville, 1965.

5 MILLER, C. William. "A Bibliographical Study of *Parthenissa.* . . ." *SB,* 2 (1949–50), 115–37.

6 MILLER, C. William. "A Source Note on Boyle's *The Generall."* *MLQ,* 8(1947):146–50.

7 MILLS, L. J. "The Friendship Theme in Orrery's Plays." *PMLA,* 53(1938): 795–806.

8 PAYNE, F. W. "The Question of Precedence between Dryden and the Earl of Orrery with regard to the English Heroic Play." *RES,* 1(1925):173–81.

9 SUMMERS, Montague. "Orrery's *The Tragedy of Zoroastres."* *MLR,* 12(1917):24–32.

Otway, Thomas (*1652–1685*)

10 *Complete Works,* ed. Montague Summers. 3 vols. 1927.

11 *Venice Preserved,* ed. Malcolm Kelsall. [RRestDS.] Lincoln, Neb., 1969.†

12 *Works: Plays, Poems and Love-Letters,* ed. J. C. Ghosh. 2 vols. Oxford, 1932. Repr. 1968.

13 FRIED, Gisela. *Gestalt und Funktion der Bilder im Drama Thomas Otways.* ("Palaestra," 239.) Göttingen, 1965.

14 HAM, Roswell G. *Otway and Lee: Biography from a Baroque Age.* New Haven, 1931.

15 HAUSER, David R. "Otway Preserved: Theme and Form in *Venice Preserv'd."* *SP,* 55(1958):481–93.

16 LEFÈVRE, André. "Racine en Angleterre au XVIIᵉ siècle: 'Titus and Berenice' de Thomas Otway." *RLC,* 34(1960):251–57.

1   McBURNEY, William H. "Otway's Tragic Muse Debauched: Sensuality in *Venice Preserv'd*." *JEGP*, 58(1959):380–99.

2   MOORE, John Robert. "Contemporary Satire in Otway's *Venice Preserved*." *PMLA*, 43(1928):166–81.

3   STROUP, Thomas B. "Otway's Bitter Pessimism." *MacMillan Festschrift*, pp. 54–75.

4   TAYLOR, Aline Mackenzie. *Next to Shakespeare: Otway's 'Venice Preserv'd' and 'The Orphan' and Their History on the London Stage*. Durham, N.C., 1950.

5   VANHELLEPUTTE, Michel. "Hofmannsthal und Thomas Otway: Zur Struktur des 'Geretteten Venedig.'" *RBPH*, 42(1964):926–39.

6   VAN VORIS, W. "Tragedy through Restoration Eyes: *Venice Preserv'd* in its Own Theatre." *Hermathena*, 99(1964):55–65.

7   WILLIAMS, Gordon. "The Sex-Death Motive in Otway's *Venice Preserv'd*." *Trivium*, 2(1967):59–70.

Ravenscroft, Edward (1654?–1707)

8   LANCASTER, H. C. "Calderon, Boursault, and Ravenscroft." *MLN*, 51 (1936):523–28.

9   McMANAWAY, James G. "The Copy for *The Careless Lovers*." *MLN*, 46(1931):406–09.

10   NORRIS, Edward T. "The Original of Ravenscroft's *Anatomist*, and an Anecdote of Jemmy Spiller." *MLN*, 46(1931):522–26.

11   PARSHALL, Raymond E. "The Source of Ravenscroft's *The Anatomist*." *RES*, 12(1936):328–33.

Settle, Elkanah (1648–1724)

12   *The Preface to "Ibrahim"* [1677], ed. Hugh Macdonald. (Luttrell Society Reprints.) Oxford, 1947.

13   BROWN, Frank C. *Elkanah Settle: His Life and Works*. Chicago, 1910.

14   DOYLE, Anne. "Dryden's Authorship of *Notes and Observations on The Empress of Morocco* (1674)." *SEL*, 6(1966):421–45.

15   DUNKIN, Paul S. "Issues of *The Fairy Queen*, 1692." *The Library*, 4th ser., 26(1946):297–304.

16   HAM, Roswell G. "The Authorship of *A Session of the Poets* (1677)." *RES*, 9(1933):319–22.

17   HAM, Roswell G. "Dryden versus Settle." *MP*, 25(1928):400–416.

1   HAVILAND, Thomas P. "Elkanah Settle and the Least Heroic Romance." *MLQ*, 15(1954):118–24. [*Ibrahim.*]

2   McFADDEN, George. "Elkanah Settle and the Genesis of *Mac Flecknoe.*" *PQ*, 43(1964):55–72.

3   NOVAK, Maximillian E., ed. "*The Express of Morocco*" *and Its Critics*. (ARS.) Los Angeles, 1968.

Shadwell, Thomas (*1642–1692*)
(See also Dryden, *Mac Flecknoe.*)

4   *Complete Works*, ed. Montague Summers. 5 vols. 1927.

5   *Epsom Wells* and *The Volunteers, or The Stock-Jobbers*, ed. D. M. Walmsley. New York, 1930.

6   "Songs and Masques in 'The Tempest' [c. 1674]," ed. J. G. McManaway. *Theatre Miscellany: Six Pieces Connected with the Seventeenth-Century Stage.* Oxford, 1953, pp. 69–96.

7   *The Virtuoso*, ed. Marjorie H. Nicolson and David S. Rodes. (RRestDS.) Lincoln, Neb., 1966.

8   ALSSID, Michael W. *Thomas Shadwell*. New York, 1967.

9   BORGMAN, Albert S. *Thomas Shadwell: His Life and Comedies*. New York, 1928.

10   LLOYD, Claude. "Shadwell and the Virtuosi." *PMLA*, 44(1929):472–94.

11   MILTON, William M. "*Tempest* in a Teapot." *ELH*, 14(1947):207–18.

12   SMITH, John Harrington. "Shadwell, the Ladies, and Change in Comedy." *MP*, 46(1948):22–33.

13   SORELIUS, Gunnar. "Shadwell Deviating into Sense: *Timon of Athens* and the Duke of Buckingham." *SN*, 36(1964):232–44.

14   STROUP, Thomas B. "Shadwell's Use of Hobbes." *SP*, 35(1938):405–32.

15   VERNON, P. F. "Social Satire in Shadwell's *Timon*." *SN*, 35(1963):221–26.

16   WALMSLEY, D. M. "Shadwell and the Operatic *Tempest*." *RES*, 2(1926): 463–66. [See further, G. Thorn-Drury, *RES*, 3(1927):204–8; and D. M. Walmsley, *RES*, 3(1927):451–53.]

17   WARD, Charles E. "*The Tempest:* A Restoration Opera Problem." *ELH*, 13(1946):119–30.

Southerne, Thomas (*1659–1746*)

18   BOWERS, Fredson. "The Supposed Cancel in Southern's *The Disappointment* Reconsidered." *The Library*, 5th ser., 5(1950):140–49.

1 DODDS, John Wendell. *Thomas Southerne, Dramatist*. New Haven, 1933.

2 HAMELIUS, Paul. "The Source of Southerne's 'Fatal Marriage.'" *MLR*, 4(1909):352–56. [See also Montague Summers, ibid., 11(1916):149–55.]

3 LEECH, Clifford. "The Political 'Disloyalty' of Thomas Southerne." *MLR*, 28(1933):421–30.

Vanbrugh, Sir John (1664–1726)

4 *Complete Works: The Plays*, ed. by Bonamy Dobrée; *The Letters*, ed. by Geoffrey Webb. 4 vols. 1927–28.

BIBLIOGRAPHY

5 HARRIS, Bernard. *Sir John Vanbrugh*. (WTW.) 1967.

6 BARNARD, John. "Sir John Vanbrugh: Two Unpublished Letters." *HLQ*, 29(1966):347–52.

7 DOBRÉE, Bonamy. *Essays in Biography, 1680–1726*. 1925. [Pp. 57–195: "The Architect of Blenheim."]

8 HODGES, John C. "The Authorship of *Squire Trelooby*." *RES*, 4(1928): 404–13.

9 MUESCHKE, Paul, and Jeanette FLEISHER. "A Re-evaluation of Vanbrugh." *PMLA*, 49(1934):848–89.

10 PATTERSON, Frank M. "The Revised Scenes of *The Provok'd Wife*." *ELN*, 4(1966):19–23.

11 ROSENBERG, Albert. "New Light on Vanbrugh." *PQ*, 45(1966):603–13.

12 SHIPLEY, John B. "The Authorship of *The Cornish Squire*." *PQ*, 47(1968): 145–56.

13 WHISTLER, Laurence. *Sir John Vanbrugh, Architect and Dramatist, 1664–1726*. 1938.

Wycherley, William (1640?–1716)

14 *Complete Works*, ed. Montague Summers. 4 vols. 1924.

15 *Complete Plays*, ed. Gerald Weales. New York, 1967.†

16 *The Country Wife*, ed. Thomas H. Fujimura. (RRestDS.) Lincoln, Neb., 1965.†

17 *The Country Wife*, ed. Steven H. Rubin. San Francisco, 1961.†

1 *The Country Wife*, ed. Ursula Todd-Naylor. Northampton, Mass., 1931.
2 *The Plain Dealer*, ed. Leo Hughes. (RRestDS.) Lincoln, Neb., 1967.†

BIBLIOGRAPHY

3 VERNON, P. F. *William Wycherley*. [WTW.] 1965.

4 AUFFRET, J. "The Man of Mode and The Plain Dealer: Common Origin and Parallels." *EA*, 19(1966):209–22.

5 AUFFRET, J. "Wycherley et ses maîtres les moralistes." *EA*, 15(1962):375–88.

6 AVERY, Emmett L. "*The Country Wife* in the Eighteenth Century." *RS*, 10(1942):142–72.

7 AVERY, Emmett L. "*The Plain Dealer* in the Eighteenth Century." *RS*, 11 (1943):234–56.

8 AVERY, Emmett L. "The Reputation of Wycherley's Comedies as Stage Plays in the Eighteenth Century." *RS*, 12(1944):131–54.

9 BERMAN, Ronald. "The Ethic of *The Country Wife*." *TSLL*, 9(1967):47–55.

10 BOWMAN, John S. "Dance, Chant, and Mask in the Plays of Wycherley." *DramS*, 3(1963):181–205.

11 CHORNEY, Alexander H. "Wycherley's Manly Reinterpretated." *Campbell Festschrift*, pp. 161–69.

12 CHURCHILL, George B. "The Originality of William Wycherley." *Schelling Anniversary Papers*, New York, 1923, pp. 65–85.

13 CONNELY, Willard. *Brawny Wycherley: First Master in English Modern Comedy*. New York, 1930.

14 CRAIK, T. W. "Some Aspects of Satire in Wycherley's Plays." *ES*, 41(1960): 168–79.

15 DONALDSON, Ian. " 'Tables Turned': *The Plain Dealer*." *EIC*, 17(1967): 304–21.

16 FRIEDSON, A. M. "Wycherley and Molière: Satirical Point of View in *The Plain Dealer*." *MP*, 64(1967):189–97.

17 KORNINGER, Siegfried. "Wycherleys satirische Methode." *WBEP*, 66 (1958):110–26.

18 MORRISSEY, L. J. "Wycherley's *Country Dance*." *SEL*, 8(1968):415–29. [*The Country Wife*.]

19 MUKHERJEE, Sujit. "Marriage as Punishment in the Plays of Wycherley." *REL*, 7(1966):61–64.

20 O'REGAN, M. J. "Furetière and Wycherley." *MLR*, 53(1958):77–81. [*Le Roman bourgeois* and *The Plain Dealer*.]

21 PERROMAT, Charles. *William Wycherley: Sa vie, son oeuvre.* 1921.

1 RIGHTER, Anne. "William Wycherley." *Restoration Theatre*, ed. John Russell Brown and Bernard Harris. (Stratford-upon-Avon Studies, 6.) London and New York, 1965), pp. 71–91.

2 ROGERS, K. M. "Fatal Inconsistency: Wycherley and *The Plain Dealer*." *ELH*, 28(1961):148–62.

3 RUNDLE, James U. "Wycherley and Calderón: A Source for *Love in a Wood*." *PMLA*, 64(1949):701–07.

4 SWANDEN, Homer. "Morality in the Theater: *The Country Wife*." *California English Journal*, 1(1965):17–24.

5 TAYLOR, Archer. "Proverbs in the Plays of William Wycherley." *Southern Folklore Quarterly*, 21(1957):213–17.

6 VERNON, P. F. "Wycherley's First Comedy and Its Spanish Source." *CL*, 18(1966):132–44. [*Love in a Wood*.]

7 VIETH, David M. "Wycherley's *The Country Wife*: An Anatomy of Masculinity." *PLL*, 2(1966):335–50.

8 VINCENT, Howard P. "The Death of William Wycherley." *HSNPL*, 15(1933):219–42.

9 VINCENT, Howard P. "William Wycherley's *Miscellany Poems*." *PQ*, 16 (1937):145–48.

10 WILLIAMS, Edwin E. "Furetière and Wycherley: 'Le Roman bourgeois' in Restoration Comedy." *MLN*, 53(1938):98–104.

11 WOLPER, Roy S. "The Temper of *The Country Wife*." *Humanities Association Bulletin*, 18(1967):69–74.

12 WOOTEN, Carl. "*The Country Wife* and Contemporary Comedy: A World Apart." *DramS*, 2(1963):333–43.

13 ZIMBARDO, Rose A. *Wycherley's Drama: A Link in the Development of English Satire*. New Haven, 1965.

Fine Arts

Painting, Sculpture, Architecture

14 ALLEN, B. Sprague. *Tides in English Taste (1619–1800): A Background for the Study of Literature*. 2 vols. Cambridge, Mass., 1937.

15 COLVIN, Howard M. *A Biographical Dictionary of English Architects, 1660–1840*. 1954.

16 EVANS, Joan. *Patterns: A Study of Ornament in Western Europe from 1180 to 1900*. 2 vols. Oxford, 1931.

17 FÜRST, Viktor. *The Architecture of Sir Christopher Wren*. 1956.

18 GREEN, David. *Grinling Gibbons: His Work as Carver and Statuary, 1648–1721*. 1964.

19 GUNNIS, Rupert. *Dictionary of British Sculptors, 1660–1851*. 1953.

50 FINE ARTS

1 HAGSTRUM, Jean H. *The Sister Arts: The Tradition of Literary Pictorialism and English Poetry from Dryden to Gray.* Chicago, 1958.

2 IRWIN, David. *English Neoclassical Art: Studies in Inspiration and Taste.* 1966.

3 KILLANIN, Michael Morris, Lord. *Sir Godfrey Kneller and His Times, 1646–1723.* 1948.

4 LINDSEY, John. *Wren: His Work and Times.* 1951.

5 PIPER, David. *Catalogue of Seventeenth-Century Portraits in the National Portrait Gallery, 1625–1714.* Cambridge, 1963.

6 SUMMERSON, John. *Sir Christopher Wren.* London and New York, 1953.

7 WHINNEY, Margaret, and Oliver MILLAR. *Oxford History of English Art.* Vol. VIII: *English Art, 1625–1714.* Oxford, 1957.

8 WHISTLER, Laurence. *The Imagination of Vanbrugh and His Fellow Artists.* 1954.

Gardening

9 FOX, Helen M. *André le Nôtre, Garden Architect to Kings.* 1963.

10 GOTHEIN, Marie Luise. *A History of Garden Art,* ed. Walter P. Wright and trans. by Mrs. Archer-Hind. 2 vols. 1928.

11 HADFIELD, Miles. *Gardening in Britain.* 1960.

12 HYAMS, Edward. *The English Garden.* 1964.†

13 OGDEN, Henry V. S., and Margaret S. *English Taste in Landscape in the Seventeenth Century.* Ann Arbor, 1955.

Music

BIBLIOGRAPHY

14 DAY, Cyrus L., and Eleanore B. MURRIE. *English Song-Books, 1651–1702: A Bibliography, with a First-Line Index of Songs.* Oxford, 1940.

15 KING, A. Hyatt. "Recent Works in Music Bibliography." *The Library,* 4th ser., 26(1945):122–48.

16 DOLMETSCH, Arnold. *The Interpretation of the Music of the XVII and XVIII Centuries, Revealed by Contemporary Evidence.* 1944.

17 DUCKLES, Vincent, and Franklin B. ZIMMERMAN. *Words to Music: Papers on English Seventeenth-Century Song.* Los Angeles, 1967.

1 HOLLAND, A. K. *Henry Purcell: The English Musical Tradition.* 1932.

2 HOLST, Imogen, ed. *Henry Purcell, 1659–1695: Essays on His Music.* 1959.

3 HUMPHRIES, Charles, and William C. SMITH. *Music Publishing in the British Isles.* 1954.

4 LAMSON, Roy, Jr. "Henry Purcell's Dramatic Songs and the English Broadside Ballad." *PMLA,* 53((1938):148–61.

5 MELLERS, Wilfrid. *Harmonious Meeting: A Study of the Relationship between English Music, Poetry and Theatre, c. 1600–1900.* 1965.

6 PARRY, C. Hubert H. *Oxford History of Music.* Vol. III: *The Music of the Seventeenth Century.* 2nd ed. Oxford, 1938.

7 PHILLIPS, James E., and Bertrand H. BRONSON. *Music and Literature in England in the Seventeenth and Eighteenth Centuries.* Los Angeles, 1953.

8 SIMPSON, Claude M. *The British Broadside Ballad and Its Music.* New Brunswick, N.J., 1966.

9 ZIMMERMAN, Franklin B. *Henry Purcell, 1659–1695.* 1967.

Philosophy

General Studies

10 BREDVOLD, Louis I. "The Invention of the Ethical Calculus." *Jones Festschrift,* pp. 165–80.

11 FRANTZ, R. W. *The English Traveller and the Movement of Ideas, 1660–1732.* Lincoln, Neb., 1934.

12 GOUGH, J. W. *The Social Contract. A Critical Study of Its Development.* Oxford, 1936. 2nd ed., 1957.

13 HAZARD, Paul. *La Crise de la conscience européenne (1680–1715).* 3 vols. 1935. [Trans. by J. Lewis May: *The European Mind: The Critical Years (1680–1715).* London and New Haven, 1953.]†

14 JONES, R. F. "The Humanistic Defence of Learning in the Mid-Seventeenth Century." *Nicolson Festschrift,* pp. 71–92.

15 KLIGER, Samuel. *The Goths in England: A Study in Seventeenth and Eighteenth Century Thought.* Cambridge, Mass., 1952.

16 LOVEJOY, Arthur O. *The Great Chain of Being: A Study of the History of an Idea.* Cambridge, Mass., 1936.†

17 LOVEJOY, Arthur O. *Essays in the History of Ideas.* Baltimore, 1948.†

18 MACKLEM, Michael. *The Anatomy of the World: Relations between Natural and Moral Law from Donne to Pope.* Minneapolis, 1958.

19 MAZZEO, Joseph A. *Renaissance and Revolution: The Remaking of English Thought.* New York, 1965.

1 NICOLSON, Marjorie. "The Early Stage of Cartesianism in England." *SP*, 26(1929):356–74.

2 NUSSBAUM, Frederick L. *The Triumph of Science and Reason, 1660–1685*. New York, 1953.

3 RANDALL, John H., Jr. *The Making of the Modern Mind: A Survey of the Intellectual Background of the Present Age*. Boston, 1926.

4 SAMS, Henry W. "Anti-Stoicism in Seventeenth- and Early Eighteenth-Century England." *SP*, 41(1944):65–78.

5 SIMON, Irène. " 'Pride of Reason' in the Restoration and Earlier Eighteenth Century." *RLV*, 25(1959):375–96, 453–73.

6 SMITH, Harold Wendell. " 'Reason' and the Restoration Ethos." *Scrutiny*, 18(1951):118–36.

7 SMITH, Preserved. *A History of Modern Culture*. Vol. I: *The Great Renewal, 1543–1687*. New York and London, 1930.†

8 STRUCK, Wilhelm. *Der Einfluss Jakob Boehmes auf die englische Literatur des 17. Jahrhunderts*. Berlin, 1936.

9 VAN LEEUWEN, Henry G. *The Problem of Certainty in English Thought, 1630–1690*. The Hague, 1963.

10 WILEY, Margaret L. *The Subtle Knot: Creative Scepticism in Seventeenth-Century England*. Cambridge, Mass., 1952.

11 WILLEY, Basil. *The Seventeenth Century Background: Studies in the Thought of the Age in Relation to Poetry and Religion*. 1934.†

The Cambridge Platonists

12 *The Cambridge Platonists, Being Selections from the Writings of Benjamin Whichcote, John Smith and Nathanael Culverwel*. With Introduction by E. T. Campagnac. Oxford, 1901.

13 *Conway Letters. The Correspondence of Anne, Viscountess Conway, Henry More, and Their Friends, 1642–1684*, ed. Marjorie Hope Nicolson. New Haven, 1930.

14 CASSIRER, Ernst. *Die Platonische Renaissance in England und die Schule von Cambridge*. Leipzig, 1932. [English trans. by James P. Pettegrove. London and Austin, Texas, 1953.]

15 COLIE, Rosalie L. *Light and Enlightenment: A Study of the Cambridge Platonists and the Dutch Arminians*. Cambridge, 1957.

16 DE BOER, John J. *The Theory of Knowledge of the Cambridge Platonists*. (Columbia Diss.) Madras, 1931.

17 FENN, Percy T., Jr. "The Latitudinarians and Toleration." *Washington University Studies, Humanistic Series*, Vol. 13, No. 1 (1925), pp. 181–245.

1   GEORGE, Edward A. *Seventeenth Century Men of Latitude.* London and New York, 1908.

2   LAMPRECHT, Sterling P. "Innate Ideas in the Cambridge Platonists." *Philosophical Review,* 35(1926):553–73.

3   MUIRHEAD, John H. *The Platonic Tradition in Anglo-Saxon Philosophy: Studies in the History of Idealism in England and America.* 1931.

4   NICOLSON, Marjorie. "Christ's College and the Latitude-Men." *MP,* 27 (1929):35–53.

5   NICOLSON, Marjorie. "George Keith and the Cambridge Platonists." *Philosophical Review,* 39(1930):36–55.

6   PAWSON, G. P. H. *The Cambridge Platonists and Their Place in Religious Thought.* 1930.

7   PINTO, V. de Sola. *Peter Sterry: Platonist and Puritan, 1613–1672: A Biographical and Critical Study with Passages Selected from His Writings.* Cambridge, 1934.

8   POWICKE, Frederick J. *The Cambridge Platonists.* 1926; Cambridge, Mass., 1927.

9   SAVESON, J. E. "Descartes' Influence on John Smith, Cambridge Platonist." *JHI,* 20(1959):258–63.

10 SAVESON, J. E. "Differing Reactions to Descartes among the Cambridge Platonists." *JHI,* 21(1960):560–67.

11 SCUPHOLME, A. C. "John Smith, a Cambridge Platonist." *Theology,* 42(1941):26–34.

12 THOMPSON, Elbert N. S. "Mysticism in Seventeenth-Century English Literature." *SP,* 18(1921)170–231.

The Idea of Progress

13 BAILLIE, John. *The Belief in Progress.* 1950.

14 BARON, Hans. "The *Querelle* of the Ancients and the Moderns as a Problem for Renaissance Scholarship." *JHI,* 20(1959):3–22.

15 BURY, J. B. *The Idea of Progress: An Inquiry into Its Origin and Growth.* 1920; New York, 1932.†

16 CRANE, R. S. "Shifting Definitions and Evaluations of the Humanities from the Renaissance to the Present." *The Idea of the Humanities and Other Essays Critical and Historical* (Chicago, 1967), I, 16–170. [See esp. pp. 72–89: "The Quarrel of the Ancients and Moderns and Its Consequences."]

17 DELVAILLE, Jules. *Essai sur l'histoire de l'idée de progrès jusqu'à la fin du XVIIIᵉ siècle.* 1910.

18 GILLOT, H[ubert]. *La Querelle des anciens et des modernes en France: De la "Défense et Illustration de la langue française" aux "Parallèles des anciens et des modernes."* 1914.

19 GINSBERG, M[orris]. *The Idea of Progress: A Revaluation.* 1953.

1 GUYER, Foster E. " 'C'est nous qui sommes les anciens.' " *MLN*, 26(1921): 257–64.

2 GUYER, Foster E. "The Dwarf on the Giant's Shoulders." *MLN*, 45(1930): 398–402.

3 HARRIS, Victor. *All Coherence Gone: The Seventeenth-Century Controversy on the Decay of Nature—A Turning Point in Modern Literary History.* Chicago, 1949.

4 JONES, Richard F. *Ancients and Moderns: A Study of the Background of the "Battle of the Books."* St. Louis, 1936. 2nd ed.: *Ancients and Moderns: A Study of the Rise of the Scientific Movement in Seventeenth-Century England.* St. Louis, 1961.†

5 RIGAULT, Hippolyte. *Histoire de la querelle des anciens et des modernes.* 1856.

6 TUVESON, Ernest L. *Millenium and Utopia: A Study in the Background of the Idea of Progress.* Berkeley, 1949.†

7 WAGER, W. Warren. "Modern Views of the Origins of the Idea of Progress." *JHI*, 28(1967):55–70.

Cudworth, Ralph (1617–1688)

8 CARRÉ, Meyrick H. "Ralph Cudworth." *Philosophical Quarterly*, 3(1953): 342–51.

9 GYSI, Lydia. *Platonism and Cartesianism in the Philosophy of Ralph Cudworth.* Bern and Oxford, 1962.

10 JACQUOT, Jean. "Le Platonisme de Ralph Cudworth." *Revue Philosophique*, 154(1964):29–44.

11 PASSMORE, J. A. *Ralph Cudworth: An Interpretation.* Cambridge, 1951.

12 SAILOR, Danton B. "Cudworth and Descartes." *JHI*, 23(1962):133–40.

Glanvill, Joseph (1636–1680)

13 *Plus Ultra, or The Progress and Advancement of Knowledge since the Days of Aristotle* (1668), ed. Jackson I. Cope. (SF&R.) Gainesville, Fla., 1958.

14 COPE, Jackson I. *Joseph Glanvill: Anglican Apologist.* St. Louis, 1956.

15 KROOK, Dorothea. "Two Baconians: Robert Boyle and Joseph Glavill." *HLQ*, 18(1955):261–78.

1 POPKIN, Richard H. "Joseph Glanvill: A Precursor of David Hume." *JHI*, 14(1953):292–303.

2 POPKIN, Richard H. "The Development of the Philosophical Reputation of Joseph Glanvill." *JHI*, 15(1954):305–11.

3 PRIOR, Moody E. "Joseph Glanvill, Witchcraft, and Seventeenth-Century Science." *MP*, 30(1932):167–93.

Hobbes, Thomas (*1588–1679*)

4 *De Cive, or The Citizen*, ed. Sterling P. Lamprecht. New York, 1949.†

5 *The Elements of Law, Natural and Politic*, ed. Ferdinand Tönnies. *To which are subjoined Selected Extracts from Unprinted MSS of Thomas Hobbes*. Cambridge, 1928.

6 *Leviathan*, ed. A. D. Lindsay. (EL.) 1914. New ed., 1950.

7 *Leviathan*, ed. Michael Oakeshott. Oxford, 1946.

BIBLIOGRAPHY

8 JESSOP, T. E. *Thomas Hobbes*. (WTW.) 1961.

9 MACDONALD, Hugh, and Mary HARGREAVES. *Thomas Hobbes: A Bibliography*. 1952.

10 BOWLE, John. *Hobbes and His Critics: A Study in Seventeenth-Century Constitutionalism*. 1951.

11 BRETT, R. L. "Thomas Hobbes." *Willey Festschrift*, pp. 30–54.

12 BROWN, K. C. "Hobbes's Grounds for Belief in a Deity." *Philosophy*, 37(1962):336–44.

13 BROWN, Keith C., ed. *Hobbes: Studies by Leo Strauss and Others*. Cambridge, Mass., 1965.

14 DODD, Mary C. "The Rhetorics in Molesworth's Edition of Hobbes." *MP*, 50(1952):36–42.

15 GAUTHIER, David P. *The Logic of Leviathan: The Moral and Political Theory of Thomas Hobbes*. 1969.

16 GERT, Bernard. "Hobbes and Psychological Egoism." *JHI*, 28(1967):503–20.

17 GOLDSMITH, Maurice M. *Hobbes's Science of Politics*. New York, 1966.

18 HOOD, F. C. *The Divine Politics of Thomas Hobbes: An Interpretation of "Leviathan."* Oxford, 1964.

19 JAMES, D. G. *The Life of Reason: Hobbes, Locke, Bolingbroke*. 1949.

20 KROOK, Dorothea. *Three Traditions of Moral Thought*. Cambridge, 1959.

1   LAIRD, John. *Hobbes.* 1934.

2   McNEILLY, F. S. *The Anatomy of Leviathan.* 1968.

3   MINTZ, Samuel I. *The Hunting of Leviathan: Seventeenth-Century Reactions to the Materialism and Moral Philosophy of Thomas Hobbes.* Cambridge, 1962.

4   MINTZ, Samuel I. "Hobbes on Heresy: A New Manuscript." *JHI,* 29(1968):409–14.

5   NICOLSON, Marjorie H. "Milton and Hobbes." *SP,* 23(1926):405–33.

6   ONG, Walter J. "Hobbes and Talon's Ramist Rhetoric in English." *TCBS,* 1(1951):260–69.

7   PETERS, Richard. *Hobbes.* 1956.†

8   PINTO, V. de S. "Was Hobbes an Ogre?" *EIC,* 7(1957):22–27.

9   SCHLATTER, Richard. "Thomas Hobbes and Thucydides." *JHI,* 6(1945):350–62.

10 SOULHIÉ, J., et al. *La Pensée et l'influence de Th. Hobbes.* 1936.

11 STEADMAN, John M. "*Leviathan* and Renaissance Etymology." *JHI,* 28(1967):575–76.

12 STEPHEN, Leslie. *Hobbes* (EML.) 1904.

13 STRAUSS, Leo. *The Political Philosophy of Hobbes: Its Basis and Its Genesis.* Trans. from the German MS by Elsa M. Sinclair. Oxford, 1936; Chicago and Cambridge, 1952.†

14 TAYLOR, A. E. "An Apology for Mr. Hobbes." *Seventeenth Century Studies Presented to Sir Herbert Grierson.* Oxford, 1938, pp. 129–47.

15 TAYLOR, A. E. "The Ethical Doctrine of Hobbes." *Philosophy,* 13(1938):406–24.

16 TEETER, Louis. "The Dramatic Use of Hobbes's Political Ideas." *ELH,* 3(1936):140–69.

17 THIELEMANN, L. J. "Thomas Hobbes dans l'*Encyclopédie.*" *Revue d'histoire littéraire de la France,* 51(1951):333–46.

18 THORPE, Clarence DeWitt. *The Aesthetic Theory of Thomas Hobbes. With Special Reference to His Contribution to the Psychological Approach to English Literary Criticism.* Ann Arbor, 1940.*

19 TÖNNIES, Ferdinand. *Thomas Hobbes: Leben und Lehre.* Stuttgart, 1925.

20 WARRENDER, Howard. *The Political Philosophy of Hobbes: His Theory of Obligation.* Oxford, 1957.

21 WATKINS, J. W. N. *Hobbes's System of Ideas: A Study in the Political Significance of Philosophical Theories.* 1965.

22 WATSON, George. "Hobbes and the Metaphysical Conceit." *JHI,* 16(1955):558–62. [See also T. M. Gang, ibid., 17(1956):418–21.]

23 WIKELUND, Philip R. " 'Thus I passe my time in this place': An Unpublished Letter of Thomas Hobbes." *ELN,* 6(1969):263–68.

24 WINDOLPH, F. Lyman. *Leviathan and Natural Law.* Princeton, 1951.

Locke, John (1632–1704)

1 *Correspondence of John Locke and Edward Clarke*, ed. with a Biographical Study by Benjamin Rand. Cambridge, Mass., 1927.

2 *Educational Writings*, ed. James L. Axtell. Cambridge, 1968.

3 *Epistola de Tolerantia—A Letter on Toleration.* Latin Text ed. Raymond Klibansky; English trans. with Introduction and Notes by J. W. Gough. Oxford, 1968.

4 *An Essay concerning Human Understanding*, ed. Alexander C. Fraser. 2 vols. Oxford, 1894.

5 *An Essay concerning Human Understanding*, abridged and ed. A. S. Pringle-Pattison. Oxford, 1924.

6 *An Essay concerning Human Understanding*, ed. John W. Yolton. (EL.) 2 vols. 1961.

7 *Essays on the Law of Nature*, ed. Wolfgang von Leyden. Oxford, 1954.

8 *Lettres inédites de John Locke à ses amis Nicholas Thoynard, Philippe Van Limborch et Edward Clarke*, ed. Henri Ollion and T. J. De Boer. The Hague, 1912.

9 *Locke on Politics, Religion and Education*, ed. Maurice Cranston. New York, 1965.†

10 *Locke's Travels in France, 1675–1679. As Related in His Journals, Correspondence and Other Papers*, ed. John Lough. Cambridge, 1953.

11 *Selections*, ed. Sterling P. Lamprecht. New York, 1928.†

12 *The Social Contract: Essays by Locke, Hume and Rousseau*, ed. Sir Ernest Barker. (WC.) 1947. New York, 1960.†

13 *Two Treatises of Civil Government*, ed. W. S. Carpenter. (EL.) 1924.

14 *Two Treatises of Government*, ed. Thomas I. Cook. [With Sir Robert Filmer's *Patriarcha*.] New York, 1947.†

15 *Two Treatises of Government*, ed. Peter Laslett. Cambridge, 1960, 1968.†

BIBLIOGRAPHY

16 GRANSTON, Maurice. *Locke.* (WTW.) 1961.

17 HARRISON, John, and Peter LASLETT. *The Library of John Locke.* Oxford, 1965.

18 LONG, P. *A Summary Catalogue of the Lovelace Collection of the Library of John Locke in the Bodleian Library.* Oxford, 1959.

19 LONG, P. "The Mellon Donation of Additional Manuscripts of John Locke from the Lovelace Collection." *Bodleian Library Record*, 7(1964):185–93.

20 AARON, R. I. *John Locke.* 1937. 2nd ed., 1955.*†

1 BONNO, Gabriel. *Les Relations intellectuelles de Locke avec la France.* Berkeley, 1955.

2 BONNO, Gabriel. "Locke et son traducteur français Pierre Coste, avec huit lettres inédites de Coste à Locke." *RLC*, 33(1959):161–79.

3 COLIE, Rosalie. "John Locke and the Publication of the Private." *PQ*, 45(1966):24–45.

4 COLIE, Rosalie L. "The Social Language of John Locke: A Study in the History of Ideas." *JBS*, 4(1965):29–51.

5 CRANE, R. S. "Notes on the Organization of Locke's 'Essay.' " *The Idea of the Humanities.* Chicago, 1967. I: 288–301.

6 CRANSTON, Maurice. *John Locke: A Biography.* London and New York, 1957.

7 DEWHURST, Kenneth. *John Locke (1632–1704), Physician and Philosopher: A Medical Biography with an Edition of the Medical Notes in his Journals.* 1963.

8 DUNN, John. *The Political Thought of John Locke: An Historical Account of the Argument of the "Two Treatises of Government."* Cambridge, 1969.

9 GIVNER, David A. "Scientific Preconceptions in Locke's Philosophy of Language." *JHI*, 23(1962):340–54.

10 GOUGH, J. W. *John Locke's Political Philosophy.* Oxford, 1950.

11 HAMPTON, John. "Les Traductions françaises de Locke au XVIIIᵉ siècle." *RLC*, 29(1955):240–51.

12 HEFELBOWER, S[amuel] G. *The Relation of John Locke to English Deism.* Chicago, 1918.

13 HOWELL, Wilbur S. "John Locke and the New Rhetoric." *QJS*, 53(1967):319–33.

14 JAMES, D. G. *The Life of Reason: Hobbes, Locke, Bolingbroke.* 1949.

15 JEFFREYS, M. V. C. *John Locke: Prophet of Common Sense.* 1967

16 LAMPRECHT, Sterling P. *The Moral and Political Philosophy of John Locke.* New York, 1918.

17 LE CLERC, Jean. *Lettres inédites de Le Clerc à Locke*, ed. Gabriel Bonno. Berkeley, 1959.

18 MacLEAN, Kenneth. *John Locke and English Literature of the Eighteenth Century.* New Haven, 1936.

19 NORRIS, John. *Cursory Reflections upon . . . An Essay concerning Human Understanding* (1690), ed. Gilbert D. McEwen. (ARS, 93.) Los Angeles, 1961.

20 O'CONNOR, D. J. *John Locke.* 1952.†

21 PAHL, Gretchen Graf. "John Locke as Literary Critic and Biblical Interpreter." *Campbell Festschrift*, pp. 139–57.

22 REDPATH, Theodore. "John Locke and the Rhetoric of the Second Treatise." *Willey Festschrift*, pp. 55–78.

1 SELIGER, M. *The Liberal Politics of John Locke.* 1968.

2 SMITH, Constance I. "Some Ideas of Education before Locke. " *JHI*, 23(1962):403–6.

3 STOLNITZ, Jerome. "Locke and the Categories of Value in Eighteenth-Century British Aesthetic Theory." *Philosophy*, 38(1963):40–51.

4 TUVESON, Ernest L. *The Imagination as a Means of Grace: Locke and the Aesthetics of Romanticism.* Berkeley, 1960.*

5 YOLTON, John W. "Locke and the Seventeenth-Century Logic of Ideas." *JHI*, 16(1955):431–52.

6 YOLTON, John W., ed. *John Locke: Problems and Perspectives: A Collection of New Essays.* Cambridge, 1969.

More, Henry (1614–1687)

7 *Enchiridion Ethicum: The English Translation of 1690.* [Facsimile.] New York, 1930.

8 *Enthusiasmus Triumphatus* (1662), ed. M. V. De Porte. (ARS, 118.) Los Angeles, 1966.

9 *The Philosophical Poems of Henry More, Comprising Psychozoia and Minor Poems*, ed. Geoffrey Bullough. Manchester, 1931.

10 *The Philosophical Writings of Henry More*, ed. Flora I. Mackinnon. New York, 1925.

11 GREENE, Robert A. "Henry More and Robert Boyle on the Spirit of Nature." *JHI*, 23(1962):451–74.

12 LICHTENSTEIN, Aharon. *Henry More: The Rational Theology of a Cambridge Platonist.* Cambridge, Mass., 1962.

13 NICOLSON, Marjorie H. "The Spirit World of Milton and More." *SP*, 22(1925):433–52.

Norris, John (1657–1711)

14 *Cursory Reflections upon a Book call'd, An Essay concerning Human Understanding* (1690), ed. Gilbert D. McEwen. (ARS, 93.) Los Angeles, 1961.

15 DRENNON, Herbert. "James Thomson and John Norris." *PMLA*, 53(1938):1094–101.

16 JOHNSTON, Charlotte. "Locke's *Examination of Malebranche* and John Norris." *JHI*, 19(1958):551–58.

1 MACKINNON, Flora I. *The Philosophy of John Norris of Bemerton.* (Wellesley College Monograph.) Baltimore, 1910.

2 POWICKE, Frederick J. *A Dissertation on John Norris.* 1893.

3 RYAN, John K. "John Norris: A Seventeenth Century English Thomist." *New Scholasticism,* 14(1940):109–45.

4 WALTON, Geoffrey. *Metaphysical to Augustan: Studies in Tone and Sensibility in the Seventeenth Century.* 1955.

Religion

(London is to be assumed as place of publication, unless otherwise noted.)

Bibliography

5 GILLETT, Charles Ripley. *Catalogue of the McAlpin Collection of British History and Theology (1501–1700) in the Union Theological Seminary in the City of New York.* 5 vols. New York., 1927–30.

General Studies

6 BOSHER, Robert S. *The Making of the Restoration Settlement: The Influence of the Laudians, 1649–1662.* New York and London, 1951.

7 CRAGG, G[erald] R. *From Puritanism to the Age of Reason: A Study of Changes in Religious Thought within the Church of England, 1660–1700.* Cambridge, 1950.*†

8 CRAGG, G[erald] R. *Puritanism in the Period of the Great Persecution, 1660–1688.* Cambridge, 1957.

9 KNOX, Ronald A. *Enthusiasm: A Chapter in the History of Religion, with Special Reference to the Seventeenth and Eighteenth Centuries.* Oxford, 1950.†

10 MITCHELL, W. Fraser. *English Pulpit Oratory from Andrewes to Tillotson: A Study of its Literary Aspects.* London and New York, 1932.*

11 PATRICK, Simon. *A Brief Account of the New Sect of Latitude-Men. . . .* (1662), ed. T. A. Birrell. (ARS, 100.) Los Angeles, 1963.

12 PLUM, Harry G. *Restoration Puritanism: A Study of the Growth of English Liberty.* Chapel Hill, 1943.

13 RICE, Hugh A. L. *Thomas Ken: Bishop and Non-Juror.* 1958.

14 RICHARDSON, Caroline F. *English Preachers and Preaching, 1640–1670: A Secular Study.* London and New York, 1928.

1 STRANKS, C. J. *Anglican Devotion: Studies in the Spiritual Life of the Church of England between the Reformation and the Oxford Movement.* 1961.

2 SYKES, Norman. *Old Priest and New Presbyter.* Cambridge, 1956.

3 SYKES, Norman. *From Sheldon to Secker: Aspects of English Church History, 1660–1768.* Cambridge, 1959.

4 WALKER, D[aniel] P. *The Decline of Hell: Seventeenth-Century Discussions of Eternal Torment.* Chicago, 1964.

5 WHITING, C. E. *Studies in English Puritanism from the Restoration to the Revolution, 1660–1688.* 1931. Repr. 1968.

6 WILKINSON, John T. *1662—and After. Three Centuries of English Non-Conformity.* 1962.

The Quakers

7 BARBOUR, Hugh. *The Quakers in Puritan England.* New Haven, 1964.

8 BRAITHWAITE, William C. *The Beginnings of Quakerism* [1647–1660]. 1912. 2nd ed., rev., Cambridge, 1955.

9 BRAITHWAITE, William C. *The Second Period of Quakerism* [1660–1725]. 1919. 2nd ed., prepared by Henry J. Cadbury. Cambridge, 1961.

10 COPE, Jackson I. "Seventeenth-Century Quaker Style." *PMLA*, 62(1956): 725–54.

11 DANIELOWSKI, Emma. *Die Journale der frühen Quäker: Zweiter Beitrag zur Geschichte des modernen Romans in England.* Berlin, 1921.

12 JONES, Rufus M. *The Later Periods of Quakerism* [from 1725]. 2 vols. 1921.

13 KIRBY, Ethyn W. "The Quakers' Efforts to Secure Civil and Religious Liberty, 1660–96." *JMH*, 7(1935):401–21.

14 LLOYD, Arnold. *Quaker Social History, 1669–1738.* 1950.

15 MAXFIELD, Ezra K. "The Quakers in English Stage Plays before 1800." *PMLA*, 45(1930):256–73. [Comment by J. W. Bowyer, pp. 957–58.]

16 MAXFIELD, Ezra K. "Daniel Defoe and the Quakers." *PMLA*, 47(1932): 170–90.

17 PHILIPS, Edith. "French Interest in Quakers before Voltaire." *PMLA*, 45(1930):238–55.

18 PHILIPS, Edith. *The Good Quaker in French Legend.* Philadelphia, 1932.

19 RAISTRICK, Arthur. *Quakers in Science and Industry: Being an Account of the Quaker Contributions to Science and Industry during the Seventeenth and Eighteenth Centuries.* 1950.

20 ROSS, Isabel. *Margaret Fell, Mother of Quakerism.* 1949.

21 RUSSELL, Elbert. *A History of Quakerism.* New York, 1942.

1 WRIGHT, Luella M. *The Literary Life of the Early Friends, 1650–1725.* New York, 1932.

2 WRIGHT, Luella M. *Literature and Education in Early Quakerism.* (University of Iowa Studies, Humanistic Series, Vol. V No. 2.) Iowa City, 1933.

Allestree, Richard (1619–1681)

3 ELMEN, Paul. "Richard Allestree and *The Whole Duty of Man.*" *The Library*, 5th ser., 6(1951):19–27.

Barrow, Isaac (1630–1677)

4 OSMOND, Percy H. *Isaac Barrow: His Life and Times.* 1944.

5 SIMON, Irène. *Three Restoration Divines: Barrow, South, Tillotson. Selected Sermons.* Vol. I. Paris, 1967. [Pp. 303–510: Texts of six sermons by Barrow.]

6 SIMON, Irène. "Tillotson's Barrow." *ES*, 45(1964):193–211, 274–88.

Baxter, Richard (1615–1691)

7 *The Autobiography of Richard Baxter, Being the Reliquiae Baxterianae abridged from the Folio (1696),* ed. J. M. Lloyd Thomas. London and New York, 1925.

8 *Devotions and Prayers of Richard Baxter,* ed. Leonard T. Grant. Grand Rapids, Mich., 1964.†

9 *Richard Baxter and Margaret Charlton: A Puritan Love-Story. Being the Breviate of the Life of Margaret Baxter, 1681.* With an Introductory Essay, Notes, and Appendices by John T. Wilkinson. 1928.

10 ABERNATHY, George R., Jr. "Richard Baxter and the Cromwellian Church." *HLQ*, 24(1961):215–31.

11 MARTIN, Hugh. *Puritanism and Richard Baxter.* 1954.

12 MOORE, Katharine. *Richard Baxter: Toleration and Tyranny (1615–1691).* 1961.

13 NUTTALL, Geoffrey F. "The MS of *Reliquiae Baxterianae.*" *Journal of Ecclesiastical History*, 6(1955):73–79.

1 NUTTALL, Geoffrey F. *Richard Baxter.* 1965.

2 POWICKE, Frederick J. *A Life of the Reverend Richard Baxter.* 2 vols. London and Boston, 1924–7.

3 SCHLATTER, Richard, ed. *Richard Baxter and Puritan Politics.* New Brunswick, N.J., 1957.

Bunyan, John (1628–1688)

4 *Grace Abounding to the Chief of Sinners,* ed. Roger Sharrock. Oxford, 1962, 1966.

5 *The Holy War,* ed. John Brown. Cambridge, 1905.

6 *The Life and Death of Mr. Badman,* ed. John Brown. Cambridge, 1905.

7 *The Pilgrim's Progress from this World to that which is to come,* ed. James B. Wharey. 2nd ed., rev. by Roger Sharrock. Oxford, 1960.

8 *The Pilgrim's Progress . . . ,* ed. Roger Sharrock. 1965.†

BIBLIOGRAPHY

9 HARRISON, Frank Mott. *A Bibliography of the Works of John Bunyan.* 1932.

10 ALPAUGH, David J. "Emblem and Interpretation in *The Pilgrim's Progress. ELH,* 33(1966):299–314.

11 BRITTAIN, Vera. *In the Steps of John Bunyan: An Excursion into Puritan England.* London and New York, 1950. [American title: *Valiant Pilgrim: The Story of John Bunyan and Puritan England.*]

12 BROWN, John. *John Bunyan (1628–1688): His Life, Times and Work.* 1928. [Tercentenary Edition, rev. by Frank Mott Harrison.]

13 FORREST, James F. "Bunyan's Ignorance and the Flatterer: A Study in the Literary Art of Damnation." *SP,* 60(1963):12–22.

14 FORREST, James F. "Mercy with Her Mirror." *PQ,* 42(1963):121–26.

15 FRYE, Roland M. *God, Man and Satan. Patterns of Christian Thought and Life in "Paradise Lost," "Pilgrim's Progress," and the Great Theologians.* Princeton, 1960.

16 GOLDER, Harold. "Bunyan and Spenser." *PMLA,* 45(1930):216–37.

17 GOLDER, Harold. "Bunyan's Giant Despair." *JEGP,* 30(1931):361–78.

18 GOLDER, Harold. "Bunyan's Valley of the Shadow." *MP,* 27(1929):55–72.

1 GREAVES, Richard L. "John Bunyan and Covenant Thought in the Seventeenth Century." *Church History*, 36(1967):151–69.

2 HARRISON, G. B. *John Bunyan: A Study in Personality.* 1928.

3 KAUFMANN, U. Milo. *"The Pilgrim's Progress" and Traditions in Puritan Meditation.* New Haven, 1966.

4 LERNER, L. D. "Bunyan and the Puritan Culture." *Cambridge Journal,* 7(1954):221–42.

5 MANDEL, Barrett J. "Bunyan and the Autobiographers' Artistic Purpose." *Criticism,* 10(1968):225–43.

6 O'DONNELL, Norbert F. "Shaw, Bunyan, and Puritanism." *PMLA,* 72(1957):520–33.

7 SHARROCK, Roger. *John Bunyan.* 1954. Rev. ed., 1968.

8 SHARROCK, Roger. *John Bunyan: The Pilgrim's Progress.* 1966.

9 SMITH, David E. *John Bunyan in America.* Bloomington, Ind., 1966.

10 TALON, Henri A. *John Bunyan, l'homme et l'oeuvre.* 1948. [English trans. by Barbara Wall, *John Bunyan: The Man and His Works.* London and Cambridge, Mass., 1951.]

11 TINDALL, William York. *John Bunyan, Mechanick Preacher.* New York, 1934.

12 WATSON, M. R. "The Drama of *Grace Abounding*." *ES,* 46(1965):471–82.

13 WEST, Alick. *The Mountain in the Sunlight: Studies in Conflict and Unity.* 1958.

14 WILLCOCKS, Mary P. *Bunyan Calling: A Voice from the Seventeenth Century.* 1943.

15 WINSLOW, Ola Elizabeth. *John Bunyan.* New York, 1961.

Fox, George (1624–1691)

16 *Journal,* ed. Rufus M. Jones. New York, 1963.†

17 *Journal,* rev. ed. by John L. Nickalls. Cambridge, 1952.

18 JONES, Rufus M. *George Fox: An Autobiography.* 2 vols. Philadelphia, 1903.

19 KNIGHT, Rachel. *The Founder of Quakerism: A Psychological Study of the Mysticism of George Fox.* 1922.

20 NOBLE, Vernon. *The Man in Leather Breeches: The Life and Times of George Fox.* London and New York, 1953.

21 WILDES, Harry E. *Voice of the Lord: A Biography of George Fox.* Philadelphia, 1965.

Penn, William (*1644–1718*)

BIBLIOGRAPHY

1 SPENCE, Mary Kirk. *William Penn: A Bibliography. A Tentative List of Publications about Him and His Work*. Harrisburg, Pa., 1932.

2 BEATTY, Edward C. O. *William Penn as Social Philosopher*. New York, 1939.

3 DOBRÉE, Bonamy. *William Penn, Quaker and Pioneer*. London and Boston, 1932.

4 DUNN, Mary M. *William Penn: Politics and Conscience*. Princeton, 1967.

5 ILLICK, Joseph E. *William Penn, the Politician: His Relations with the English Government*. Ithaca, N. Y., 1965.

6 PEARE, Catherine Owens. *William Penn: A Biography*. Philadelphia, 1957.†

7 VULLIAMY, C. E. *William Penn*. 1933.

South, Robert (*1634–1716*)

8 MATTIS, Norman. "Robert South." *QJS*, 15(1929):537–60.

9 SIMON, Irène. *Three Restoration Divines: Barrow, South, Tillotson: Selected Sermons*. Vol. I. Paris, 1967.

10 SPIKER, Sina. "Figures of Speech in the Sermons of Robert South." *RES*, 16(1940):444–55.

11 SUTHERLAND, James, "Robert South." *REL*, 1(1960):5–12.

Tillotson, John (*1630–1694*)

12 BROWN, David D. "Dryden's 'Religio Laici' and the 'Judicious and Learned Friend.'" *MLR*, 56(1961):66–69.

13 BROWN, David D. "John Tillotson's Revisions and Dryden's 'Talent for English Prose.'" *RES*, n.s. 12(1961):24–39.

14 BROWN, David D. "The Text of John Tillotson's Sermons." *The Library*, 5th ser., 13(1958):18–36. [See further note, "The Dean's Dilemma," ibid., 14(1959):282–87.]

1 BROWN, David D. "Voltaire, Archbishop Tillotson, and the Invention of God." *RLC*, 34(1960):257–61.

2 LOCKE, Louis G. *Tillotson: A Study in Seventeenth-Century Literature.* ("Anglistica," IV.) Copenhagen, 1954.

3 SIMON, Irène. *Three Restoration Divines: Barrow, South, Tillotson: Selected Sermons.* Vol. I. Paris, 1967.

4 SIMON, Irène. "Tillotson's Barrow." *ES*, 45(1964):193–211, 273–88.

5 SYKES, Norman. "The Sermons of Archbishop Tillotson." *Theology*, 58(1955):297–302.

Science

Bibliography

6 "Annual Critical Bibliography of the History and Philosophy of Science." *Isis: International Review Devoted to the History of Science and Civilization.* Brussels and Berne, 1913– . [Now published by the Smithsonian Institution, Washington.]

7 DUDLEY, Fred A., and others, eds. *The Relations of Literature and Science: A Selected Bibliography, 1930–1949.* Pullman, Wash., 1949. [Continued in *Symposium.*]

General Studies

8 ARMITAGE. Angus. *Edmond Halley.* 1966.

9 BREDVOLD, Louis I. "Dryden, Hobbes, and the Royal Society." *MP*, 25(1928):417–38.

10 BURTT, Edwin A. *The Metaphysical Foundations of Modern Physical Science.* London and New York, 1925.†

11 DEWHURST, Kenneth. *Dr. Thomas Sydenham, 1624–1689: His Life and Original Writings.* London and Berkeley, 1966.

12 DEWHURST, Kenneth. *Thomas Willis as a Physician.* Los Angeles, 1964.

13 DUNCAN, C. S. *The New Science and English Literature in the Classical Period.* Menasha, Wis., 1913.

14 DUNCAN, C. S. "The Scientist as a Comic Type." *MP*, 14(1916):281–91.

15 FEISENBERGER, H. A. "The Libraries of Newton, Hooke, and Boyle." *Notes and Records of the Royal Society of London*, 21(1966):42–55.

16 FISCH, H., and H. W. JONES. "Bacon's Influence on Sprat's *History of the Royal Society.*" *MLQ*, 12(1951):399–406.

17 GUNTHER, R. T. *Early Science in Cambridge.* Oxford, 1937.

1 HALL, Arthur R. *The Scientific Revolution, 1500–1800: The Foundation of the Modern Scientific Attitude.* 1954.†

2 HALLEY, Edmond. *Correspondence and Papers*, ed. Eugene F. MacPike. Oxford, 1932.

3 HARRISON, Charles T. "Bacon, Hobbes, Boyle, and the Ancient Atomists." *HSNPL*, 15(1933):191–218.

4 HOUGHTON, Walter E., Jr. "The English Virtuoso in the Seventeenth Century." *JHI*, 3(1942):51–73, 190–219.

5 JONES, Richard F. *Ancients and Moderns: A Study of the Rise of the Scientific Movement in Seventeenth Century England.* 2nd ed., rev. St. Louis, 1961.*†

6 JONES, Richard F. "The Rhetoric of Science in England of the Mid-Seventeenth Century." *McKillop Festschrift*, pp. 5–24.

7 JONES, Richard F. "Science and Criticism in the Neo-Classical Age of English Literature." *JHI*, 1(1940):381–412.

8 JONES, Richard F. "Science and English Prose Style in the Third Quarter of the Seventeenth Century." *PMLA*, 45(1930):977–1009. [Repr. in *Jones Festschrift*.]

9 JONES, Richard F. "Science and Language in England of the Mid-Seventeenth Century." *JEGP*, 31(1932):315–31. [Repr. in *Jones Festschrift*.]

10 LLOYD, Claude. "Shadwell and the Virtuosi." *PMLA*, 44(1929):472–94.

11 LYONS, Henry. *The Royal Society, 1660–1940: A History of its Administration under its Charters.* Cambridge, 1944.

12 MacPIKE, Eugene F. *Dr. Edmond Halley (1656–1742): A Bibliographical Guide to his Life and Work. . . .* 1939.

13 MEYER, Gerald D. *The Scientific Lady in England, 1650–1760. . . .* Berkeley, 1955.

14 NICOLSON, Marjorie H. "English Almanacs and the 'New Astronomy.'" *AS*, 4(1939):1–33.

15 NICOLSON, Marjorie H. *The Microscope and English Imagination.* (Smith College Studies in Modern Languages, Vol. 16, No. 4. 1935. [Repr. in *Science and Imagination*. Ithaca, N.Y., 1956.]

16 NICOLSON, Marjorie H. "Milton and the Telescope." *ELH*, 2(1935):1–32.

17 NICOLSON, Marjorie H. "The 'New Astronomy' and English Literary Imagination." *SP*, 32(1935):428–62.

18 NICOLSON, Marjorie H. "The Telescope and Imagination." *MP*, 32(1935): 233–60.

19 NICOLSON, Marjorie H. *A World in the Moon: A Study of the Changing Attitude toward the Moon in the Seventeenth and Eighteenth Centuries.* (Smith College Studies in Modern Languages, Vol. 17, No. 2.) 1936.

20 OLDENBURG, Henry. *Correspondence*, ed. Rupert Hall and Marie Boas Hall. Madison, Wis., 1965– . [In progress. Vol. 4: *1667–1668*, 1968.]

1 ORNSTEIN, Martha. *The Role of Scientific Societies in the Seventeenth Century.* Chicago, 1913. Repr. 1928.

2 PURVER, Margery. *The Royal Society: Concept and Creation.* Cambridge, Mass., 1967.

3 SILVETTE, Herbert. *The Doctor on the Stage: Medicine and Medical Men in Seventeenth Century England.* Nashville, 1967.

4 SIMPSON, H. C. "The Vogue of Science in English Literature, 1600–1800." *UTQ,* 2(1933):143–67.

5 SINGER, Charles, E. J. HOLMYARD, and Trevor I. WILLIAMS, eds. *A History of Technology.* Vol. III: *From the Renaissance to the Industrial Revolution.* Oxford, 1957.

6 SPRAT, Thomas. *History of the Royal Society,* ed. Jackson I. Cope and Harold W. Jones. St. Louis, 1958.

7 STIMSON, Dorothy. *Scientists and Amateurs: A History of the Royal Society.* 1949.

8 THORNDIKE, Lynn. *A History of Magic and Experimental Science.* Vols. VII–VIII: *The Seventeenth Century.* New York, 1958.

9 WESTFALL, Richard S. *Science and Religion in Seventeenth-Century England.* New Haven, 1958.

10 WOLF, A. *A History of Science, Technology, and Philosophy in the Sixteenth and Seventeenth Centuries.* 1935.

Boyle, Robert (*1627–1691*)

BIBLIOGRAPHY

11 FULTON, John F. *A Bibliography of the Honourable Robert Boyle, Fellow of the Royal Society.* Oxford, 1961.

12 BOAS, Marie. *Robert Boyle and Seventeenth-Century Chemistry.* Cambridge, 1958.

13 FISCH, Harold. "The Scientist as Priest: A Note on Robert Boyle's Natural Theology." *Isis,* 44(1953):252–65.

14 FISHER, Mitchell S. *Robert Boyle, Devout Naturalist: A Study in Science and Religion in the Seventeenth Century.* Philadelphia, 1945.

15 FULTON, J. F. "Robert Boyle and His Influence on Thought in the Seventeenth Century." *Isis,* 18(1932):77–102.

16 GREENE, Robert A. "Henry More and Robert Boyle on the Spirit of Nature." *JHI,* 23(1962):451–74. [See also William Appelbaum, "Boyle and Hobbes: A Reconsideration." *JHI,* 25(1964):117–19.]

17 HALL, Marie Boas. *Robert Boyle on Natural Philosophy: An Essay, with Selections from His Writings.* Bloomington, Ind., 1965.

1 KARGON, Robert. "Walter Charleton, Robert Boyle, and the Acceptance of Epicurean Atomism in England." *Isis*, 55(1964):184–92.

2 KROOK, Dorothea. "Two Baconians: Robert Boyle and Joseph Glanvill." *HLQ*, 18 (1955):261–78.

3 LOEMKER, Leroy E. "Boyle and Leibniz." *JHI*, 16(1955):22–43.

4 MORE, Louis T. *The Life and Works of the Honourable Robert Boyle.* 1944.

5 O'BRIEN, John J. "Samuel Hartlib's Influence on Robert Boyle's Scientific Development." *AS*, 21(1965):1–14, 257–76.

6 WESTFALL, Richard S. "Unpublished Boyle Papers Relating to Scientific Method." *AS*, 12(1956):63–73; 103–17.

Burnet, Thomas (1635?–1715)

7 *The Sacred Theory of the Earth.* Introduction by Basil Willey. (Centaur Classics.) London and Carbondale, Ill., 1965.

8 HALLER, Elizabeth. *Die barocken Stilmerkmale in der englischen, lateinischen, und deutschen Fassung von Dr. Thomas Burnets "Theory of the Earth."* Bern, 1940.

9 OGDEN, H. V. S. "Thomas Burnet's *Telluris theoria sacra* and Mountain Scenery." *ELH*, 14(1947):139–50.

10 TUVESON, Ernest. "The Origins of the 'Moral Sense.'" *HLQ*, 11(1948): 241–59.

Hooke, Robert (1635–1703)

11 *Diary, 1672–1680*, ed. Henry W. Robinson and Walter Adams. 1935.

BIBLIOGRAPHY

12 KEYNES, Geoffrey. *A Bibliography of Dr. Robert Hooke.* Oxford, 1960.

13 'ESPINASSE, Margaret. *Robert Hooke.* Berkeley and London, 1956.†

14 GUNTHER, R. T. *Early Science in Oxford.* Vols. VI, VII, XIII: *The Life and Work of Robert Hooke.* Oxford, 1930, 1945. Vol. VIII: *The Cutler Lectures of Robert Hooke.* Oxford, 1931.

15 WATTIE, Margaret. "Robert Hooke on His Literary Contemporaries." *RES*, 13(1937):212–16.

Newton, Sir Isaac (1642–1727)

16 *Correspondence*, ed. H. W. Turnbull and J. F. Scott. Cambridge, 1959– . Vols. I–III: *1661–1694*, ed. H. W. Turnbull (1959–61). Vol. IV: *1694–1709*, ed. J. F. Scott (1966). [In progress.]

17 *Mathematical Papers,* ed. D. T. Whiteside and others. Cambridge, 1966– . [In progress.]

18 *Newton's Mathematical Principles of Natural Philosophy and His "System of the World,"* trans. Andrew Motte (1729). Rev. and ed. Florian Cajori. 2 vols. Berkeley, 1962.

1 *Newton's Philosophy of Nature*, ed. H. S. Thayer. New York, 1953.†
2 *Opticks . . .* , with Foreword by Albert Einstein. New York, 1952.†
3 *Principia*, Vols. I, II. Berkeley, 1961–62.†

BIBLIOGRAPHY

4 GRAY, George John. *A Bibliography of the Works of Sir Isaac Newton, together with a List of Books illustrating his Works.* 2nd ed., rev. and enl. Cambridge, 1907.

5 ANDRADE, E. N. da C. *Sir Isaac Newton.* London and New York, 1954.†

6 BELL, Arthur E. *Newtonian Science.* 1961.

7 COHEN, I. Bernard. "Newton in the Light of Recent Scholarship." *Isis,* 51(1960):489–514.

8 GUERLAC, Henry. "Newton's Changing Reputation in the Eighteenth Century." *Carl Becker's "Heavenly City" Revisited,* ed. Raymond O. Rockwood. Ithaca, N.Y., 1958, pp. 3–26.

9 KOYRÉ, Alexandre. *Newtonian Studies.* Cambridge, Mass., and London, 1965.†

10 MANUEL, Frank E. *Isaac Newton, Historian.* Cambridge, Mass., 1963.

11 MANUEL, Frank E. *A Portrait of Isaac Newton.* Cambridge, Mass., 1968.

12 MORE, Louis T. *Isaac Newton: A Biography.* New York, 1934.†

13 NORTH, John D. *Isaac Newton.* 1967.

14 STRONG, E. W. "Newton and God." *JHI,* 13(1952):147–67.

15 STRONG, E. W. "Newtonian Explications of Natural Philosophy." *JHI,* 18(1957):49–83.

Ray, John (1627–1705)

BIBLIOGRAPHY

16 KEYNES, Geoffrey. *John Ray: A Bibliography.* 1951.

17 RAVEN, Charles E. *John Ray, Naturalist: His Life and Works.* Cambridge, 1942. 2nd ed., 1950.

Wilkins, John (*1614–1672*)

1 ANDRADE, E. N. da C. "The Real Character of Bishop Wilkins." *AS*, 1(1936):4–12.

2 CHRISTENSEN, Francis. "John Wilkins and the Royal Society's Reform of Prose Style." *MLQ*, 7(1946):179–87, 279–90.

3 DE MOTT, Benjamin. "Science versus Mnemonics. Notes on John Ray and on John Wilkins' *Essay towards a Real Character, and a Philosophical Language.*" *Isis*, 48(1957):3–12.

4 DE MOTT, Benjamin. "The Sources and Development of John Wilkins' 'Philosophical Language.' " *JEGP*, 57(1958):1–13.

5 EMERY, Clark. "John Wilkins and Noah's Ark." *MLQ*, 9(1948):286–91.

6 EMERY, Clark. "John Wilkins' Universal Language." *Isis*, 38(1948):174–85.

7 FUNKE, Otto. "On the Sources of John Wilkins' 'Philosophical Language' (1668)." *ES*, 40(1959):208–14.

8 FUNKE, Otto. *Zum Weltsprachenproblem in England im 17. Jahrhundert: G. Dalgarno's "Ars Signorum" (1661) und J. Wilkins' "Essay towards a Real Character and a Philosophical Language" (1668)*. Heidelberg, 1929.

9 HENDERSON, P. A. Wright. *The Life and Times of John Wilkins*. 1910.

10 KOLB, Gwin J. "Johnson's 'Dissertation on Flying' and John Wilkins' *Mathematical Magick*." *MP*, 47(1949):24–31.

11 McCOLLEY, Grant. "The Debt of Bishop John Wilkins to the *Apologia pro Galileo* of Tomaso Campanella." *AS*, 4(1939):150–68.

12 McCOLLEY, Grant. "The Ross-Wilkins Controversy. *AS*, 3(1938):153–89.

13 SHAPIRO, Barbara. *John Wilkins, 1614–1672: An Intellectual Biography*. Berkeley, 1969.*

14 SIMON, Walter G. "Comprehension in the Age of Charles II." *Church History*, 31(1962):440–48.

15 STIMSON, Dorothy. "Dr. Wilkins and the Royal Society." *JMH*, 3(1931):539–63.

Miscellaneous Prose Writers

Aubrey, John (1626–1697)

1 *Brief Lives, Chiefly of Contemporaries, . . . set down between the Years 1669 and 1696*, ed. from the Author's Manuscripts by Andrew Clark. 2 vols. Oxford, 1898.

2 *Brief Lives*, ed. Oliver L. Dick. 1949. Ann Arbor, 1957.†

3 *The Scandal and Credulities of John Aubrey*, ed. John Collier. 1931.

4 POWELL, John. *John Aubrey and His Friends*. 1948.

Brown, Thomas (1663–1704)

5 *Amusements, Serious and Comical, and Other Works*, ed. Arthur L. Hayward. London and New York, 1927.

6 BOYCE, Benjamin. *Tom Brown of Facetious Memory*. *Grub Street in the Age of Dryden*. Cambridge, Mass., 1939.

7 EDDY, William A. "Tom Brown and Partridge the Astrologer." *MP*, 28(1930):163–68.

Burnet, Gilbert (1643–1715)

8 *History of His Own Time*, ed. M. J. Routh. 7 vols. Oxford, 1823, 1833; ed. Osmund Airy (Vols. I–II only), Oxford, 1897–1900.

9 *A Supplement to Burnet's "History of My Own Time."* ed. H. C. Foxcroft. Oxford, 1902.

10 CLARKE, T. E. S., and H. C. FOXCROFT. *A Life of Gilbert Burnet, Bishop of Salisbury*. Cambridge, 1907.

11 DOBELL, R. J. "The Bibliography of Gilbert Burnet." *The Library*, 5th ser., 5(1950):61–3. [Addenda by David I. Masson, p. 151; by J. H. R. Pafford, ibid., 6 (1951):126.]

12 MOGG, W. Rees. "Some Reflections on the Bibliography of Gilbert Burnet." *The Library*, 5th ser., 4(1949):100–13.

Clarendon, Edward Hyde, Earl of (1609–1674)

1 *The History of the Rebellion and Civil Wars in England, begun in the Year 1641,* ed. W. D. Macray. 6 vols. Oxford, 1888.

2 *Selections from "The History of the Rebellion and Civil Wars" and "The Life of Himself,"* ed. G. Huehns. (WC.) 1955.

3 ABERNATHY, George R., Jr. "Clarendon and the Declaration of Indulgence." *Journal of Ecclesiastical History*, 11(1960):55–73.

4 CRAIK, Henry. *The Life of Edward, Earl of Clarendon.* 2 vols. 1911.

5 DAVIS, Herbert. "The Augustan Conception of History." *Nicolson Festschrift*, pp. 213–29.

6 FIRTH, Charles. "Clarendon's History of the Rebellion." *EHR*, 19(1904): 26–54, 246–62, 464–83.

7 FIRTH, Charles. *Edward Hyde, Earl of Clarendon as Statesman, Historian, and Chancellor of the University.* Oxford, 1909.

8 FOGLE, French R., and H. R. TREVOR-ROPER. *Milton and Clarendon. Two Papers on 17th Century English Historiography Presented at a Seminar Held at the Clark Library on December 12, 1964.* Los Angeles, 1965.

9 HARDACRE, P. H. "Portrait of a Bibliophile. I: Edward Hyde, Earl of Clarendon, 1609–74." *Book Collector*, 7(1958):361–68.

Davenant, Charles (1656–1714)

10 DAVIES, Godfrey, and Marjorie SCOFIELD. "Letters of Charles Davenant." *HLQ*, 4(1941):309–42.

11 WADDELL, David. "The Writings of Charles Davenant (1656–1714)." *The Library*, 5th ser., 11(1956):206–12.

12 WADDELL, David. "Charles Davenant (1656–1714): A Biographical Sketch." *Economic History Review*, 2nd ser., 11(1958):279–88.

Evelyn, John (1620–1706)

13 *Diary*, ed. E. S. De Beer. 6 vols. Oxford, 1955. (One-volume text: Oxford, 1959.)

1   *Diary*. (EL.) 2 vols. 1952. Rev. ed., 1966. [Text of William Bray ed.]

2   *Life of Mrs. Godolphin*, ed. Harriet Sampson. 1939.

3   *Memoires for My Grand-Son*, ed. Geoffrey Keynes. 1926.

4   *Tyrannus, or the Mode* (1661), ed. J. L. Nevinson. (Luttrell Society Reprints.) Oxford, 1951.

BIBLIOGRAPHY

5   KEYNES, Geoffrey. *John Evelyn: A Study in Bibliophily: A Bibliography of His Writings*. Cambridge and New York, 1937. 2nd ed. Oxford, 1968.

6   WILLY, Margaret. *English Diarists: Evelyn and Pepys*. (WTW.) 1963.

7   BOAS, Guy. "John Evelyn, 'Virtuoso': In the Light of Recent Research." *EDH*, n.s. 28(1956):106–22.

8   DENNY, Margaret. "The Early Program of the Royal Society and John Evelyn." *MLQ*, 1(1940):481–97.

9   HISCOCK, W. G. *John Evelyn and Mrs. Godolphin*. 1951.

10   HISCOCK, W. G. *John Evelyn and His Family Circle*. 1955.

11   MARBURG, Clara. *Mr. Pepys and Mr. Evelyn*. Philadelphia, 1935.

12   O'MALLEY, C. D. "John Evelyn and Medicine." *Medical History*, 12(1968): 219–31.

13   PARKS, George B. "John Evelyn and the Art of Travel." *HLQ*, 10(1947): 251–76.

14   PONSONBY, Arthur. *John Evelyn, Fellow of the Royal Society, Author of "Sylva."* 1933.

Halifax, Sir George Savile, Marquis of (*1633–1695*)

15   *Complete Works*, ed. J. P. Kenyon. 1969.†

16   *Complete Works*, ed. Sir Walter Raleigh. Oxford, 1912.

17   *The Lady's New Year Gift; or Advice to a Daughter*, ed. Bonamy Dobrée. 1927.

18   BENSON, Donald R. "Halifax and the Trimmers." *HLQ*, 27(1964):115–34.

19   FOXCROFT, H. C. *A Character of the Trimmer, Being a Short Life of the First Marquis of Halifax*. Rev. ed. Cambridge, 1947.

1 GATHORNE-HARDY, Robert. "Halifax's *The Character of a Trimmer:*
Some Observations in the Light of a Manuscript from Ickworth." *The
Library*, 5th ser., 14(1959):117–23.

2 NEWCOMB, Robert. "Poor Richard's Debt to Lord Halifax." *PMLA,*
70(1955):535–39.

3 PAGLIARO, Harold E. "Paradox in the Aphorisms of La Rochefoucauld
and Some Representative English Followers." *PMLA*, 79(1964):42–50.

Harrington, James (*1611–1677*)

4 *Political Writings*, ed. Charles Blitzer. Indianapolis, 1955.†

5 BLITZER, Charles. *An Immortal Commonwealth: The Political Thought of
James Harrington.* New Haven, 1960.

6 MACPHERSON, C[rawford] B. *The Political Theory of Possessive Indi-
vidualism: Hobbes to Locke.* Oxford, 1962.†

7 SHKLAR, Judith N. "Ideology Hunting: The Case of James Harrington."
American Political Science Review, 53(1959):662–92.

8 TAWNEY, Richard H. "Harrington's Interpretation of His Age." *PBA,*
27(1944):199–223.

9 WATSON, George. "James Harrington: A Last Apology for Poetry."
MLN, 71(1956):170–72.

L'Estrange, Sir Roger (*1616–1704*)

10 *Citt and Bumpkin* (1680), ed. B. J. Rahn. (ARS, 117.) Los Angeles, 1965.

11 KETTON-CREMER, R. W. "A Letter of Sir Roger L'Estrange." *TLS,*
March 13, 1959, p. 152.

12 KITCHIN, George. *Sir Roger L'Estrange: A Contribution to the History of
the Press in the Seventeenth Century.* 1913.

Newcastle, Margaret Cavendish, Duchess of (*1623–1673*)

13 *The Life of William Cavendish, Duke of Newcastle, to which is added The True
Relation of My Birth, Breeding and Life*, by Margaret, Duchess of Newcastle,
ed. C. H. Firth. 1886. (EL.) 1915.

14 *The Phanseys of William Cavendish, Marquis of Newcastle, Addressed to
Margaret Lucas, and Her Letters in Reply*, ed. Douglas Grant. 1956.

1 GAGEN, Jean. "Honor and Fame in the Works of the Duchess of Newcastle." *SP*, 56(1959):519–38.

2 GRANT, Douglas. *Margaret the First: A Biography of Margaret Cavendish, Duchess of Newcastle, 1623–1673.* 1956.

3 MINTZ, Samuel I. "The Duchess of Newcastle's Visit to the Royal Society." *JEGP*, 51(1952):168–76.

Pepys, Samuel (*1633–1703*)

4 *Charles II's Escape from Worcester*, ed. William Matthews. Berkeley, 1967.

5 *Diary*, ed. Robert Latham and William Matthews. London and Berkeley, 1970– .

6 *Diary*, abr. and ed. by O. F. Morshead (*Everybody's Pepys*). Illus. by Ernest H. Shepard. London and New York, 1926.†

7 *Diary*, abr. and ed. John Warrington. (EL.) 3 vols. 1953. (Text of Mynors Bright, 1875–79.)

8 *Diary*, ed. Henry B. Wheatley. 10 vols. 1893–99.

9 *The Letters of Samuel Pepys and His Family Circle*, ed. Helen Truesdell Heath. Oxford, 1955. [See also G. S. Rousseau, "Two New Pepys Letters." *RES*, n.s. 19(1968):169–72.]

10 *Private Correspondence and Miscellaneous Papers*, ed. J. R. Tanner. 2 vols. London and New York, 1926.

11 *Samuel Pepys's Naval Minutes*, ed. J. R. Tanner. 1926.

BIBLIOGRAPHY

12 WILLY, Margaret. *English Diarists: Evelyn and Pepys.* (WTW.) 1963.

13 BRYANT, Arthur. *Samuel Pepys: The Man in the Making.* Cambridge, 1933. New ed., London, 1947.

14 BRYANT, Arthur. *Samuel Pepys: The Years of Peril.* Cambridge, 1935.

15 BRYANT, Arthur. *Samuel Pepys: The Saviour of the Navy.* Cambridge. 1938.

16 EMDEN, Cecil S. *Pepys Himself.* New York, 1963.

17 EMSLIE, Macdonald. "Pepys's Songs and Songbooks in the Diary Period." *The Library*, 5th ser., 12(1957):240–55.

18 HUNT, Percival. *Samuel Pepys in the Diary.* Pittsburgh, 1958.

19 MARBURG, Clara. *Mr. Pepys and Mr. Evelyn.* Philadelphia, 1935.

20 MATTHEWS, A. G. *Mr. Pepys and Nonconformity.* 1954.

1 MATTHEWS, William. "Pepys's Transcribers." *JEGP*, 34(1935):213–24.

2 MENDELSOHN, Oscar A. *Drinking with Pepys.* 1963.

3 NICOLSON, Marjorie H. *Pepys' "Diary" and the New Science.* Charlottesville, 1965.

4 PONSONBY, Arthur. *Samuel Pepys.* (EML.) 1928.

5 TANNER, J. R. *Mr. Pepys: An Introduction to the Diary, Together with a Sketch of His Later Life.* 1925.

6 TAYLOR, Ivan E. *Samuel Pepys.* New York, 1967.

7 WILSON, John Harold. *The Private Life of Mr. Pepys.* New York, 1959.

Petty, Sir William (*1623–1687*)

8 *The Petty Papers: Some Unpublished Writings of Sir William Petty*, ed. the Marquis of Lansdowne. 2 vols. 1927.

9 *Petty-Southwell Correspondence, 1676–1687*, ed. the Marquis of Lansdowne. 1928.

10 FITZMAURICE, Edmond G. P. F. *The Life of Sir William Petty, 1623–1687.* 1895.

11 PASQUIER, Maurice. *Sir William Petty, ses idées économiques.* 1903.

12 STRAUSS, E[rich]. *Sir William Petty: Portrait of a Genius.* 1954.

Rymer, Thomas (*1641–1713*)

13 *Critical Works*, ed. Curt A. Zimansky. New Haven, 1956.

14 ALEXANDER, Nigel. "Thomas Rymer and 'Othello.' " *Shakespeare Survey*, 21(1968):66–77.

15 DOUGLAS, David C. *English Scholars, 1660–1730.* 1939. Rev. ed., 1951.

16 STOLL, E. E. "*Oedipus* and *Othello*: Corneille, Rymer and Voltaire." *RAA*, 12(1935):385–400.

17 WALCOTT, Fred G. "John Dryden's Answer to Thomas Rymer's *The Tragedies of the Last Age*." *PQ*, 15(1936):194–214.

18 WATSON, George. "Dryden's First Answer to Rymer." *RES*, n.s. 14(1963): 17–23.

Saint-Evremond, Charles de Marguetel de Saint Denis de (1613?–1703)

1 *Oeuvres en prose*, ed. René Ternois. Vols. I–III. 1963–66.

2 *Saint-Evremond, Critique Littéraire*, ed. Maurice Wilmotte. 1921.

3 *Letters*, ed. John Hayward. 1930.

4 ADEN, John M. "Dryden and Saint-Evremond." *CL*, 6(1954):232–39.

5 BARNWELL, H. T. *Les Idées morales et critiques de Saint-Evremond.* 1957.

6 DANIELS, Walter M. *Saint-Evremond en Angleterre.* Versailles, 1907.

7 HOPE, Quentin M. *Saint-Evremond: The Honnête Homme as Critic.* Bloomington, Ind., 1962.

8 JOLIAT, Eugène. "L'Auteur malgré lui." *UTQ*, 25(1955):154–66.

9 LOWENS, Irving. "St. Evremond, Dryden, and the Theory of Opera." *Criticism*, 1(1959):226–48.

10 POTTS, D. C. "Desmaizeaux and Saint-Evremond's Text." *French Studies*, 19(1965):239–52.

11 POTTS, D. C. "Saint-Evremond's Exile and the First Edition of his *Oeuvres meslées.*" *French Studies*, 21(1967):312–18.

12 THOMSON, D. W. "Saint-Evremond and Longinus." *MLN*, 51(1936):10–17.

Temple, Sir William (1628–1699)

13 *The Early Essays and Romances of Sir William Temple, Bt., with the Life and Character of Sir William Temple by His Sister, Lady Giffard*, ed. G. C. Moore Smith. Oxford, 1930.

14 "An Essay upon the Original and Nature of Government" (from *Miscellanea*), ed. Robert C. Steensma. (ARS, 109.) Los Angeles, 1964.

15 *Five Miscellaneous Essays by Sir William Temple*, ed. Samuel H. Monk. Ann Arbor, 1963.

16 *The Letters of Dorothy Osborne to Sir William Temple*, ed. G. C. Moore Smith. Oxford, 1928.

17 HALEWOOD, William H. "Young William Temple and Young Jonathan Swift." *CLAJ*, 10(1966):105–13.

1 LONGE, Julia G. *Martha Lady Giffard: Her Life and Correspondence (1664–1722), a Sequel to the Letters of Dorothy Osborne.* 1911.

2 MARBURG, Clara. *Sir William Temple: A Seventeenth Century "Libertin."* New Haven, 1932.

3 ROBERTS, William. "Sir William Temple on Orinda: Neglected Publications." *PBSA,* 57(1963):328–36.

4 WOODBRIDGE, Homer E. *Sir William Temple: The Man and His Work.* New York, 1940.

Wood, Anthony (1632–1695)

5 *Life and Times . . . , collected from His Diaries and Other Papers,* by Andrew Clark. 5 vols. Oxford, 1891–1900.

6 FRENCH, J. Milton. "The Reliability of Anthony Wood and Milton's Oxford M. A." *PMLA,* 75(1960):22–30.

7 PARKER, William R. "Wood's Life of Milton: Its Sources and Significance." *PBSA,* 52(1958):1–22.

8 SOMMERLAD, M. J. "The Continuation of Anthony Wood's *Athenae Oxonienses.*" *Bodleian Library Record,* 7(1966):264–71.

NOTES

INDEX OF AUTHORS

AUTHORS B–D

Duckles, Vincent, 50.17
Dudley, Fred A., 65.7
Duncan, C. S., 66.13, 66.14
Dunkin, Paul S., 45.15
Dunn, John, 58.8
Dunn, Mary M., 65.4
Dust, Alvin I., 40.4

Eddy, William A., 72.7
Eidson, J. O., 20.13
Einstein, Albert, 70.2
Eliot, T. S., 9.6, 9.7
Elledge, Scott, 4.11
Ellis, Amanda M., 13.9, 20.14
Ellis, William D., Jr., 41.4
Elmen, Paul, 62.3
Emden, Cecil S., 76.16
Emerson, Oliver F., 9.8, 9.9
Emery, Clark, 71.5, 71.6
Emslie, Macdonald, 9.10, 9.11, 76.17
Enck, John J., 17: note
Erskine-Hill, Howard, 5.8, 28.5
'Espinasse, Margaret, 69.13
Evans, G. Blakemore, 13.10, 13.11
Evans, Joan, 49.16
Evans, Robert O., 6.19
Evans, Willa McClung, 26.1
Ewald, Alexander C., 38.2

Farmer, A. J., 42.15
Feder, Lillian, 20.15
Feil, J. P., 40.5
Feiling, Keith, 2.10
Feisenberger, H. A., 66.15
Fenn, Percy T., Jr., 52.17
Ferry, Anne Davidson, 11.15, 17.5
Firth, Charles H., 2.14, 73.6, 73.7, 75.13
Fisch, Harold, 7.1, 66.16, 68.13
Fisher, Mitchell S., 68.14
Fitzmaurice, Edmond G. P. F., 77.10
Fleisher, Jeannette, 47.9
Flower, Margaret, 29.13
Fogle, French R., 73.8
Ford, Boris, 1.9
Forrest, James F., 63.13, 63.14
Forsythe, Robert S., 41.5
Fowler, Alastair, 14.11
Fox, Helen, M., 50.9
Foxcroft, H. C., 72.9, 72.10, 74.19
Foxell, Nigel, 14.12
Frantz, R. W., 51.11
Fraser, Alexander C., 57.4
Freedman, Morris, 9.12, 11.16, 20.16

Freeman, Phyllis, 30.11–14
French, A. L., 11.17
French, J. Milton, 79.6
Fried, Gisela, 44.13
Friedson, A. M., 48.16
Frost, William, 22.9
Frye, Roland M., 63.15
Fujimura, Thomas H., 14.5, 15.22, 28.6, 34.3, 42.2, 47.16
Fulton, John F., 68.11, 68.15
Funke, Otto, 71.7, 71.8
Furber, Elizabeth C., 3.2
Fürst, Viktor, 49.17
Fussell, G. E., 3.10

Gagen, Jean E., 16.1, 34.4, 38.13, 76.1
Gale, Cedric, 37.8
Gallagher, Mary, 22.10
Gallaway, Francis, 5.9
Gardner, William B., 8.5, 9.13
Garnett, Richard, 1.10
Gathorne-Hardy, Robert, 75.1
Gatto, Louis C., 20.17
Gauthier, David P., 55.15
George, Edward A., 53.1
Gert, Bernard, 55.16
Ghosh, J. C., 44.12
Gibbs, A. M., 40.6
Gibson, Dan, 25.7
Giddey, Ernest, 28.7
Gillett, Charles Ripley, 60.5
Gillot, Hubert, 53.18
Ginsberg, Morris, 53.19
Givner, David A., 58.9
Goggin, L. P., 17.6
Golden, Samuel, 30.6, 30.7
Golder, Harold, 63.16–18
Goldgar, Bertrand A., 23.15
Goldsmith, Maurice M., 55.17
Gosse, Anthony, 38.14, 38.15
Gosse, Edmund, 5.10, 27.7, 38.16
Gothein, Marie Luise, 50.10
Gough, J. W., 51.12, 57.3, 58.10
Graham, C. B., 41.6
Grant, Douglas, 75.14, 76.2
Grant, Leonard T., 62.8
Gray, George John, 70.4
Greaves, Richard L., 64.1
Green, David, 49.18
Greene, Donald J., 1.4
Greene, Robert A., 59.11, 68.16
Grierson, H. J. C., 1.11
Griffith, Ben, 17: note
Grose, Clyde L., 2.11

91

AUTHORS G—J

Guerlac, Henry, 70.8
Guilhamet, Leon M., 11.18
Gunn, J. A. W., 2.12
Gunnis, Rupert, 49.19
Gunther, R. T., 66.17, 69.14
Guyer, Foster E., 54.1, 54.2
Gysi, Lydia. 54.9

Hadfield, Miles, 50.11
Hagstrum, Jean H., 23.16, 50.1
Halewood, William H., 78.17
Haley, K. H. D., 2.13
Hall, Arthur R., 67.1
Hall, Marie Boas, 67.20, 68.17
Hall, Rupert, 67.20
Haller, Elizabeth, 69.8
Halley, Edmond, 67.2
Ham, Roswell G., 9.14, 28.8; 43.10, 44.14, 45.16, 45.17
Hamelius, Paul, 47.2
Hamilton, Kenneth G., 5.11, 9.15, 23.17
Hamilton, Marion H., 19.5, 19.6
Hamm, Victor M., 13.1, 14.6
Hammond, H., 11.19
Hampton, John, 58.11
Harbage, Alfred, 32.2, 32.3, 40.7
Hardacre, P. H., 73.9
Hargreaves, Mary, 55.9
Harris, Bernard, 16.4, 35.6, 35.21, 36.2, 39.5, 47.5, 49.1
Harris, Brice, 26.5
Harris, Victor, 54.3
Harrison, Charles T., 67.3
Harrison, Frank Mott, 63.9, 63.12
Harrison, G. B., 64.2
Harrison, John, 57.17
Harth, Phillip, 9.16
Hartsock, Mildred E., 16.2
Hathaway, Baxter, 20.18
Hauser, David R., 44.15
Haviland, Thomas P., 46.1
Haycraft, Howard, 1.12
Hayman, John G., 23.18, 42.3
Hayward, Arthur L., 72.5
Hayward, John, 27.10, 78.3
Hazard, Paul, 51.13
Hazlitt, William, 34.5
Heath, Helen Truesdell, 76.9
Hefelbower, Samuel G., 58.12
Hemphill, George, 9.17
Henderson, P. A. Wright, 71.9
Hinnant, Charles H., 14.13
Hiscock, W. G., 74.9, 74.10

Hochuli, Hans, 37.3
Hodges, John C., 38.8, 38.17–20, 47.8
Hoffman, Arthur W., 9.18
Hole, Christina, 3.11
Holland, A. K., 51.1
Holland, Norman H., 34.6
Hollander, John, 14.14, 24.1
Holmyard, E. J., 68.5
Holst, Imogen, 51.2
Hood, F. C., 55.18
Hook, Lucyle, 28.9, 28.10
Hooker, Edward N., 8.7, 14.7, 14.15
Hooker, Helene Maxwell, 13.2, 22.11, 26.8
Hope, A. D., 14.16
Hope, Quentin M., 78.7
Hopper, Vincent F., 42.10
Horsman, E. A., 9.19
Hotson, Leslie, 32.4
Houghton, Walter E., Jr., 67.4
Howarth, R. G., 8.2, 26.6, 38.21
Howell, Wilbur S., 58.13
Howells, A. C., 7.2
Hoy, Cyrus, 32.5
Huehns, G., 73.2
Hughes, Charlotte B., 39.17
Hughes, Leo, 48.2
Hume, Robert D., 20.19
Humphries, Charles, 51.3
Hunt, Percival, 76.18
Huntley, Frank L., 20.20, 21.1
Hussey, Richard, 26.2
Hyams, Edward, 50.12

Illick, Joseph E., 65.5
Irvine, Maurice, 26.10
Irwin, David, 50.2

Jack, Ian, 24.2
Jackson, Wallace, 17.7
Jacquot, Jean, 54.10
James, D. G., 55.19, 58.14
James, Eugene N., 42.17
Jameson, R. D., 21.2
Jeffares, A. Norman, 38.4
Jefferson, D. W., 9.20, 16.3, 16.4
Jeffreys, M. V. C., 58.15
Jenson, H. James, 21.3
Jessop, T. E., 55.8
Johnston, Charlotte, 59.16
Joliat, Eugène, 78.8
Jones, Claude E., 33.10
Jones, Harold W., 11.20, 66.16, 68.6

AUTHORS

Strong, E. W., 70.14, 70.15
Stroup, Thomas B., 43.7, 45.3, 46.14
Struck, Wilhelm, 52.8
Strunk, W., 17: head, 19: note, 19.2
Stuart, D. M., 29.8
Suckling, Norman, 17.15, 35.6
Summers, Montague, 7.14, 31.4,
  32.1, 33.3, 33.4, 38.3, 44.9, 44.10,
  46.4, 47.2, 47.14
Summerson, John, 50.6
Sutherland, James R., 2.4, 3.1, 43.2,
  65.11
Sutherland, W. O. S., Jr., 15.11
Swanden, Homer, 49.4
Swedenberg, H. T., Jr., 8.7, 10.21–23,
  11.4, 15.12
Sykes, Norman, 61.2, 61.3, 66.5

Talon, Henri A., 64.10
Tanner, J. E., 13.16
Tanner, J. R., 76.10, 76.11, 77.5
Tawney, Richard H., 75.8
Taylor, A. E., 56.14, 56.15
Taylor, Aline Mackenzie, 13.17,
  45.4
Taylor, Archer, 49.5
Taylor, D. Crane, 39.12
Taylor, Ivan E., 77.6
Teeter, Louis, 56.16
Ternois, René, 78.1
Thale, Mary, 21.18, 21.19
Thayer, H. S., 70.1
Thielemann, L. J., 56.17
Thomas, J. M. Lloyd, 62.7
Thompson, Elbert N. S., 53.12
Thomson, D. W., 78.12
Thorndike, Lynn, 68.8
Thorn-Drury, G., 13.18, 46.16
Thorpe, Clarence DeWitt, 6.3, 56.18
Thorpe, James, 27.13, 41.13
Thorson, James L., 25.16
Thurber, C. N., 43.3
Tietje, Hans, 7.11
Tillyard, E. M. W., 15.13, 21.20
Tindall, William York, 64.11
Todd, William B., 28.17
Todd-Naylor, Ursula, 48.1
Tönnies, Ferdinand, 55.5, 56.19
Towers, Tom H., 13.19
Traugott, John, 35.7
Trevor-Roper, H. R., 73.8
Trotter, Eleanor, 4.6
Trowbridge, Hoyt, 21.21, 21.22
Turnbull, H. W., 69.16

Turnell, G. M., 10.24
Turner, Darwin T., 39.13
Tuveson, Ernest L., 54.6, 59.4, 69.10

Underwood, Dale, 42.9
Ure, Peter, 18.11
Ustick, W. Lee, 4.7, 4.8

Van Doren, Mark, 10.25, 10.26
Vanhelleputte, Michel, 45.5
Van Leeuwen, Henry G., 52.9
Van Lennep, William, 32.7
Van Voris, William H., 39.14, 45.6
Vaughn, Jack A., 41.9, 41.10
Veldkamp, Jan, 25.17
Vernon, P. F., 35.8, 46.15, 48.3, 49.6
Verrall, A. W., 11.1
Vetter, Dale B., 31.2
Vieth, David M., 15.14, 23.5, 27.11,
  28.18, 49.7
Vincent, E. R., 30.3
Vincent, Howard P., 49.8, 49.9
Vines, Sherard, 6.4
Vulliamy, C. E., 65.7

Waddell, David, 73.11, 73.12
Wager, W. Warren, 54.7
Waith, Eugene M., 16.13, 16.14
Walcott, Fred G., 22.1, 77.17
Walcott, Robert, 3.2
Walker, Daniel P., 61.4
Walker, J., 4.9
Wall, Barbara, 64.10
Wallace, John M., 6.19, 11.2
Waller, A. R., 2.5, 24.19
Wallerstein, Ruth C., 12.15, 15.15,
  22.2, 24.11
Walmsley, D. M., 36.12, 46.5, 46.16
Walton, Geoffrey, 60.4
Ward, A. W., 2.5
Ward, Charles E., 8.2, 11.3, 11.4,
  14.8, 46.17
Warrender, Howard, 56.20
Warrington, John, 76.7
Wasserman, Earl R., 15.16, 15.17,
  24.12
Wasserman, George R., 11.5
Watkins, J. W. N., 56.21
Watson, George, 6.5, 19.13, 22.3,
  56.22, 75.9, 77.18
Watson, M. R., 64.12
Wattie, Margaret, 69.15
Weales, Gerald, 47.15

AUTHORS W—Z

Webb, Geoffrey, 47.4
Weinbrot, Howard D., 17.16, 24.13
Welcher, Jeanne K., 14.9
Welle, J. A. van der, 11.6
Wellington, James E., 12.16
West, Albert H., 24.14
West, Alick, 64.13
Westfall, Richard S., 68.9, 69.6
Wharey, James B., 63.7
Wheatley, Henry B., 76.8
Whinney, Margaret, 50.7
Whistler, Laurence, 47.13, 50.8
White, Arthur F., 39.19
White, Eric W., 36.13
Whiteside, D. T., 69.17
Whitfield, Francis, 28.19
Whiting, C. E., 61.5
Whiting, George W., 33.5
Wieder, Robert, 44.2
Wikelund, Philip R., 56.23
Wilcox, John, 35.9
Wilders, John, 24.20
Wildes, Harry E., 64.21
Wiles, R. M., 4.10
Wiley, Margaret L., 52.10
Wilkinson, D. R. M., 35.10
Wilkinson, John T., 61.6, 62.9
Willcocks, Mary P., 64.14
Willey, Basil, 52.11, 69.7
Williams, Aubrey, 39.15
Williams, Charles, 29.1
Williams, Edwin E., 49.10
Williams, Gordon, 45.7
Williams, T. D. Duncan, 30.10
Williams, Trevor I., 68.5
Williams, Weldon M., 27.5, 27.6

Williamson, George, 6.6, 6.7, 7.12,
   22.4, 22.5, 24.15
Willy, Margaret, 74.6, 76.12
Wilmotte, Maurice, 78.2
Wilson, Edward M., 30.3
Wilson, F. P., 7.13
Wilson, John Harold, 24.16, 27.15,
   29.2–4, 33.6–9, 35.23, 37.11, 39.16,
   77.7
Wilson, Stuart, 31.5
Windolph, F. Lyman, 56.24
Wing, Donald G., 1.1
Winship, George P., 39.20
Winslow, Ola Elizabeth, 64.15
Winterbottom, John A., 16.15–17
Wolf, A., 68.10
Wolf, J. Q., 12.17
Wolper, Roy S., 49.11
Wood, Henry, 24.17
Wood, Paul Spencer, 6.8, 6.9
Woodbridge, Homer E., 79.4
Woodward, Gertrude L., 31.6
Wooten, Carl, 49.12
Wright, Herbert G., 15.18
Wright, Luella M., 62.1, 62.2
Wright, Walter P., 50.10

Yolton, John W., 57.6, 59.5, 59.6
Young, Kenneth, 11.7
Youngren, William H., 6.10

Zebouni, Selma, 16.18
Zimansky, Curt A., 77.13
Zimbardo, Rose A., 49.13
Zimmerman, Franklin B., 50.17,
   51.9

INDEX OF SUBJECTS

SUBJECTS D–K

Desmaizeaux, Pierre, 78.10
Dialogue, 7.9
Dillon, Wentworth. *See* Roscommon
Donne, John, 18.10, 40.6, 51.18
Dorset, Charles Sackville, Earl of, 26.4–7
Downes, John, 32.1
Draghi, Giovanni Battista, 14.10
Drama, 31.3 ff, 56.16, 61.15, 68.3
Dryden, John, 7.14 ff, 14.20, 30.13, 35.11, 35.18, 43.4, 44.8, 66.9, 78.4
Duffett, Thomas, 36.1
D'Urfey, Thomas, 40.13 ff
Duval, Claude, 25.1

Eccles, John, 36.9
Education, 3.7, 3.13, 4.5, 57.2, 57.9, 59.2, 62.2
Egoism, 55.16
Emblems, 63.10
Encyclopédie, 56.17
Enthusiasm, 6.7, 59.8, 60.9
Epicureanism, 69.1
Epicurus, 14.7
Etherege, Sir George, 34.6, 41.14 ff
Evelyn, John, 73.13 ff

Fame, 76.1
Family, 4.4
Farquhar, George, 34.5, 42.12 ff
Fell, Margaret, 61.20
Figures of speech, 65.10
Filmer, Sir Robert, 9.21, 57.14
Fine arts, 49.14 ff
Flecknoe, Richard, 41.20
Fox, George, 64.16–21
France, 57.10, 58.1, 58.2, 58.11, 61.17, 61.18
Franklin, Benjamin, 75.2
French sources, 24.9, 24.14, 30.2, 35.3
Friendship, 44.7
Furetière, Antoine, 48.21, 49.10

Gafori, Franchino, 15.10
Gardening, 50.9–13
Gay, John, 41.4
Generality, 6.10
Gibbons, Grinling, 49.18
Giffard, Martha, Lady, 78.13, 79.1
Glanvill, Joseph, 54.13 ff
Godolphin, Margaret Blagge, 74.2, 74.9
Goodman, Cardell, 33.7

Granville, George, Lord Lansdowne, 35.3, 36.4
Grub Street, 72.6

Halifax, Charles Montagu, Earl of, 26.8, 26.9
Halifax, George Savile, Marquis of, 74.15 ff
Halley, Edmond, 66.8, 67.12
Hannibal, 14.19
Harrington, James, 75.4–9
Hartlib, Samuel, 69.5
Hell, 61.4
Herculean hero, 16.13
Heroic play, 35.11 ff
Hewitt, John, 35.3
History, 11.2, 73.5, 73.8
Hobbes, Thomas, 16.16, 30.4, 40.3, 46.14, 55.4, ff, 66.9, 67.3, 68.16, 75.6
Hofmannsthal, Hugo von, 45.5
Holidays, 3.17
Holland, 11.6, 52.15
Honor, 16.1, 76.1
Hooke, Robert, 66.15, 69.11–15
Horace, 13.9, 20.14, 21.11
Housewife, 3.11
Howard, Sir Robert, 18.13, 43.3–6
Hume, David, 55.1, 57.12
Hyde, Edward. *See* Clarendon
Hymns, 8.1

Imagery, 9.10, 9.18, 9.20, 15.11, 17.11
Imagination, 4.15, 20.6, 50.8, 59.4, 67.15, 67.17, 67.18
Imitation, 21.6, 21.18, 23.12
Industry, 61.19
Invention, 9.3
Irony, 15.14
Italian sources, 30.3

Johnson, Samuel, 71.10
Jonson, Ben, 27.6, 32.11, 41.6
Journalism, 4.9, 44.2, 75.12
Juvenal, 21.11

Keith, George, 53.5
Ken, Thomas, 60.13
Killigrew, Anne, 14.16, 15.3, 15.14, 15.15
K[irke], E[dward], 15.10
Kneller, Sir Godfrey, 50.3
Knights, L. C., 34.7

Language, 6.10, 7.5, 7.6, 58.4, 58.9, 67.9, 71.3, 71.4, 71.6–8
Lansdowne, Lord. *See* Granville
La Ramée, Pierre de. *See* Ramus
La Rochefoucauld, François, duc de, 75.3
Latitudinarians, 52.12 ff, 60.11
Laureateship, 30.6
Lawes, Henry, 26.1
Le Clerc, Jean, 58.17
Lee, Nathaniel, 35.11, 43.7–10
Leibniz, G. W., 69.3
Le Nôtre, André, 50.9
L'Estrange, Sir Roger, 75.10–12
Libertinism, 33.20, 79.2
Liberty, 60.12
Libraries, private, 38.19, 57.17, 66.15
Lillo, George, 17.7
Limborch, Philippe van, 57.8
Lipsius, Justus, 6.14, 6.18
Locke, John, 57.1 ff, 59.16, 75.6
Longinus, 21.6, 78.12
Lucas, Margaret. *See* Newcastle
Lucian, 9.4
Lucretius, 22.10

Machiavelli, 11.22
Magic, 68.8
Maintenon, Françoise d'Aubigné, marquise de, 26.7
Malebranche, Nicolas, 59.16
Marlowe, Christopher, 16.13
Marprelate, Martin, 12.18
Marriage, 48.19
Marvell, Andrew, 11.17
May, Thomas, 17.2
Medicine, 58.7, 68.3, 74.12
Metaphysical poetry, 5.19, 6.5, 56.22
Microscope, 67.15
Millenium, 54.6
Milton, John, 5.17, 67.16, 79.6, 79.7; and Bunyan, 63.15; and Clarendon, 73.8; and Dryden, 9.12, 11.10, 11.15, 19.8, 20.16, 22.5; and Etherege, 42.4; and Hobbes, 56.5; and More, 59.13
Mnemonics, 71.3
Molière, Jean Baptiste Poquelin, 33.10, 34.14, 35.6, 35.9, 48.16
Molloy, Charles, 35.3
Monmouth, Duke of, 11.23
Montaigne, Michel Eyquem de, 6.14
Montagu, Charles. *See* Halifax
Moon, 67.19

Moral sense, 69.10
More, Henry, 52.13, 59.7–13
Motteux, Peter Anthony, 43.11 ff
Mountfort, William, 31.9
Mountain scenery, 69.9
Mulgrave, John Sheffield, Earl of, 26.10
Muret, Marc-Antoine, 6.19
Music, 9.23, 12.3, 15.2, 24.1, 50.14 ff
Mysticism, 53.12

Nature, 54.3, 57.7, 68.16
Newcastle, Margaret Cavendish, Duchess of, 75.13 ff
Newcastle, William Cavendish, Duke of, 75.13, 75.14
Newton, Sir Isaac, 66.15, 69.16 ff
Nonconformity, 3.13, 4.5, 61.6, 76.20
Norris, John, 59.14 ff

Oldenburg, Henry, 67.20
Oldham, John, 15.6, 27.1–6
Opera, 21.5, 36.8–13, 46.6, 46.11, 46.16, 46.17
Orrery, Roger Boyle, Earl of, 35.11, 35.18, 44.3–9
Osborne, Dorothy, 78.16
Otway, Thomas, 44.10 ff
Oxenden, Sir George, 25.13
Oxford University, 69.14, 73.7

Painting, 31.2, 49.14 ff
Panegyric, 9.22, 23.13
Paradox, 75.3
Parody, 24.3
Partridge, John, 72.7
Penn, William, 65.1–7
Pepys, Samuel, 33.3, 76.4 ff
Petty, Sir William, 77.9–13
Philips, Ambrose, 41.4
Philips, Katherine, 27.7–9, 79.3
Philosophy, 51.10 ff, 68.10
Pix, Mary, 35.3
Platonism, 35.18, 40.12, 54.9, 54.10
Platonists, Cambridge, 52.12 ff
Poetical justice, 39.15
Poetry, 23.1 ff, 75.9
Politics, 13.5, 23.10, 55.17, 55.18, 57.9, 59.1, 63.3
Pope, Alexander, 9.3, 41.4, 51.18
Popish plot, 12.11
Preaching, 7.3, 60.10, 60.14
Préciosité, 33.16, 33.20, 40.12
Printers, 4.1

101

SUBJECTS P–S

Probability, 33.17
Progress, idea of, 10.3, 55.13 ff
Prologues and epilogues, 8.5, 15.9, 31.8
Prose style, 6.11 ff, 10.17, 10.20
Prosody, 8.15
Proverbs, 49.5
Puns, 33.18
Puppets, 33.2
Purcell, Henry, 32.9, 51.1, 51.2, 51.4, 51.9
Puritanism, 4.4, 7.1, 60.7, 60.8, 60.12, 61.5, 62.11, 63.3, 64.3, 64.4, 64.6

Quakers, 61.7 ff
Quinault, Philippe, 19.3

Racine, Jean, 44.16
Raillery, 23.18, 34.1
Ramus, Petrus (Pierre de La Ramée), 56.6
Ravenscroft, Edward, 45.8–11
Ray, John, 70.16, 70.17, 71.3
Reason, 5.9, 5.15, 52.2, 52.5, 52.6, 55.19
Religion, 9.24, 10.24, 23.2, 57.9, 60.5 ff, 68.9, 68.13, 68.14, 71.14
Rhetoric, 14.4, 20.15, 31.8, 55.14, 56.6, 58.13, 58.22, 67.6
Rhyme, 20.16
Rochester, John Wilmot, Earl of, 10.9, 27.10 ff
Romanticism, 59.4
Roscommon, Wentworth Dillon, Earl of, 29.5–8
Ross, Alexander, 71.12
Rousseau, Jean-Jacques, 57.12
Royal Society, 6.13, 66.9, 66.16, 67.11, 68, 2, 68.6. 68.7, 71.15, 74.8, 76.3
Rules, 21.12, 21.15, 21.22
Rymer, Thomas, 77.13–18

Sackville, Charles. See Dorset
Saint-Amant, Marc Antoine Gérard, sieur de, 24.8, 27.8
Saint-Evremond, Charles de Marguetel de Saint Denis de, 78.1–12
Sallust, 12.10
Satire: in poetry, 23.5, 23.8, 23.13, 23.15, 23.18, 24.2, 24.10, 24.13; in Butler, 25.11; in Dryden, 11.10, 11.11; Mulgrave's essay upon, 26.10; in Oldham, 27.4–6; in

Rochester, 28.4, 28.6, 28.12, 28.13; in plays, 33.5, 34.12; in Congreve, 38.12; in Otway, 45.2; in Shadwell, 46.15; in Wycherley, 48.14, 48.16, 48.17, 49.13
Savile, Sir George. See Halifax
Savile, Henry, 27.14
Scepticism, 14.3, 43.6, 52.10
Science, 6.10, 24.6, 52.2, 55.3, 61.19, 66.6 ff, 77.3
Scipio, 14.19
Sculpture, 49.14 ff
Secker, Thomas, 61.3
Sedley, Sir Charles, 17.1, 17.3, 29.9–11
Seneca, 7.12
Sentimental comedy, 41.8
Serial publication, 4.10
Servants, 39.13
Settle, Elkanah, 35.11, 45.12 ff
Seymour, Edward, 12.9
Shadwell, Thomas, 35.3, 46.4–17
Shaftesbury, Anthony Ashley Cooper, 1st Earl of, 2.13, 12.15
Shakespeare, William, 16.13; adaptations of, 36.1–7; and Davenant, 40.10, 40.11; and Dryden, 17.10, 17.14, 20.13, 21.8, 22.2; and Rymer, 77.15, 77.17; and Shadwell, 46.6, 46.11, 46.13, 46.15; and Tate, 30.4, 30.5, 30.9, 30.10
Shaw, George Bernard, 64.6
Sheldon, Gilbert, 61.3
Sheridan, Richard Brinsley, 37.8
Simon, Richard, 14.8
Simplicity, 5.12
Smith, John, 52.12, 53.9, 53.11
Social and cultural background, 3.3 ff
Social contract, 51.12, 57.12
Songs, 8.6, 32.12–14, 35.19, 36.11, 40.13, 41.17, 46.6, 50.14, 50.17, 51.4, 76.17
South, Robert, 65.8–11
Southerne, Thomas, 46.18 ff
Southwell, Sir Robert, 77.10
Spanish sources, 16.7, 30.3, 49.6
Spectator, The, 30.12
Spenser, Edmund, 15.10, 18.10, 63.16
Spiller, Jeremy, 45.10
Sprat, Thomas, 66.16
Stanley, Thomas, 29.12 ff
Sterry, Peter, 53.7
Stoicism, 16.17